Life as Liberty,
Life as Trust

Life as Liberty,
Life as Trust

Edited by

J. Robert Nelson

William B. Eerdmans Publishing Company
Grand Rapids, Michigan

ISBN 0-8028-0637-6

Contents

Preface

IT IS SELF-EVIDENT, wrote the young Thomas Jefferson, that "life, liberty, and the pursuit of happiness" are divinely bestowed endowments for all persons. Most people, according to polls, believe that "life is a gift of God" and therefore possesses inherent sacredness, a belief that is also upheld by the Christian faith. It is also a basic biblical teaching that liberty of life is given to humans, *liberty* meaning both liberation from sin and the state of being free. The third Jeffersonian endowment, however, is not wholly recognized by the Christian faith as an essential gift. The "pursuit of happiness" is too hedonistic to belong to this triad. In place of it Christians recognize trust or faithfulness. Like freedom, *trust* has two meanings: both trust in God's mercies and trustworthiness in the stewardship of the gifts of life and freedom.

The writers of the following essays have reflected very soberly on the meaning of the formulation "Life as Liberty, Life as Trust" as it pertains to certain urgent problems of human life. How can strong beliefs in human freedom and responsible trust in God motivate people to correct the calamitous conditions of poverty, the vicious attitudes of racism, and the lethal scourge of malnutrition and famine? How can the powers of the new genetic technology be prevented from causing injury and injustice rather than health and equity? Holding these discussions together, like theological bookends, are the chapters on God's life-giving mercies and their promises of irrepressible hope.

Addressing their thoughts to these questions are six persons of high reputation and tested credentials. Robert Jewett is Professor of New Testament Interpretation at Garrett-Evangelical Theological Seminary in Evanston, Illinois. He is both a leading expert on the letters of St. Paul and an informed critic of American culture.

James Wallis founded the inner-city Sojourners Community in Washington, D.C., and the well-known journal *Sojourners.* He participates frequently in activities related to the problems of poverty and oppression in various countries.

Bishop Roy Sano of the United Methodist Church in Denver, Colorado, speaks and acts consistently for all who suffer the consequences of racism, and especially for persons of Asian and Pacific Islander descent.

As a teacher of law and former U.S. congressman, Robert F. Drinan, S.J., has been an advocate and defender of human rights for many years. He is Professor of Law at Georgetown University, Washington, D.C.

The professional interests of J. Robert Nelson are threefold: the ecumenical movement, systematic theology, and bioethics. Since 1985 he has been the director of the Institute of Religion at the Texas Medical Center in Houston.

Gabriel Fackre, an effective interpreter of theology to both scholars and laity, is the Abbot Professor of Christian Theology at Andover Newton Theological School, Newton Centre, Massachusetts.

All six men are recognized intellectual leaders as well as

prolific writers and active participants in religious and social movements dedicated to life, liberty, and trust. They presented these chapters as the Parker Memorial Lectures at the Institute of Religion of the Texas Medical Center in Houston.

J. Robert Nelson

"Life to the Dead" from the God of *Tender Mercies*

Robert Jewett

I exhort you therefore, brothers [and sisters],
　　through the mercies of God,
to present your bodies as a sacrifice, living, holy,
　　and acceptable to God
　　　— your reasonable worship.

Romans 12:1[1]

For this [reason it is] from faith, thus according to grace, that the promise might be guaranteed to all the descendants, not only to those of the law but also to those of the faith of Abraham, who is the father of us all, just as it is written that

　"I have made you a father of many nations"
　　— in the presence of the God in whom he had faith,

---

1. I am following here the strophic pattern suggested by Johannes Weiss, "Beiträge zur Paulinischen Rhetorik," in *Theologische Studien: Festschrift für Bernhard Weiss* (Göttingen: Vandenhoeck & Ruprecht, 1897), p. 243. Throughout this chapter I have used my own translation for Scripture quotations.

who gives life to the dead
and calls that which does not exist into being.

Romans 4:16-17[2]

IN THE FILM *Tender Mercies* and in Paul's letter to the Romans, there is a theme of considerable significance for persons involved in the mysteries of human restoration. Robert Duvall plays the role of Mac Sledge, a country western singer and composer from Texas. Down-and-out after an alcoholic binge, Sledge is taken in as a motel handyman by the young widow Rosa Lee. Tess Harper plays the role of this simple, pious woman whose steadiness and love nurses Sledge back to life. Early in the film, after he begins to regain his humanity, he writes a new song about his estranged daughter. He submits the song to his former manager and receives the message one more time that he is all washed up. Sledge responds with a profane outburst against the world. Rosa Lee replies, "It's bound to be hard on you. . . . I love you," touching his cheek tenderly. "I say my prayers for you and when I thank the Lord for his tender mercies, you're at the head of the list." These words prove significant, because Rosa Lee's prayers are ultimately answered. Mac Sledge finds himself again a musician and a stepfather.

The reference to God's tender mercies is reminiscent of Paul's letter to the Romans. In the admonition of 12:1, Paul appeals to Christians "through the mercies of God" to live out their lives in service to a world full of people like Mac Sledge, his egocentric and addicted former wife Dixie, and his doomed daughter Sue Ann. Living in response to God's mercies links Paul's letter to this screenplay by Texas playwright Horton Foote. But what is of particular interest to us today is that

2. The rhetorical structure is discussed by J. P. Louw, *A Semantic Discourse Analysis of Romans* (University of Pretoria, 1979), pp. 67-68.

such tender mercies are largely invisible. Both for Paul and for Foote's story, faith is required because the mercies of God are elusive, intangible, and off camera. In a mysterious way, the God of Abraham "gives life to the dead and calls that which does not exist into being," to use the language of Romans 4.

Can we really set our faith in such an elusive God? How can we who are committed to healing rely on mercies so ordinary that they are virtually invisible?

I

The story of Abraham in Romans 4, just like that of Sledge, centers on the provision of a future through the tender mercies of God. From the perspective of the ancient Semites, Abraham and Sarah had no future because they had grown too old to have a son. As Genesis describes them, "Abram was very rich in cattle, silver, and gold. . . . But Sarai, Abram's wife, had borne him no children" (Gen. 13:2; 16:1).[3] They were doomed to extinction because their lineage would not pass on to the next generation. Their life story would be forgotten when they died; everything they had accomplished in life would be for nought. But Abraham developed faith that the unseen God of the universe would provide them an heir. He felt that a promise had been given that a son would be born from Sarah's barren womb.[4]

Paul makes it plain that there was no proof that such a miracle would occur, and that Abraham had done nothing to guarantee it. Paul repudiates the Rabbinic dogma that "At that time the unwritten law was named among them, and the works

3. John Van Seters suggests that these two statements were linked in an early form of the Abraham story; see his *Abraham in History and Tradition* (New Haven: Yale University Press, 1975), p. 224.

4. For a discussion of the story of the birth of Isaac in the context of other ancient Near Eastern stories of divine promise of an heir for an elderly couple, see ibid., pp. 202-8.

of the commandment were then fulfilled."[5] Paul explicitly claims that Abraham's faith did not rest on the fulfillment of a commandment such as circumcision (Rom. 4:10-15). The birth would be a matter of sheer grace, unearned and undeserved. All Abraham had was faith in the promise from this invisible God — in the future mercies of an elusive deity. Thus Paul insists that the Abraham story is one of "faith, thus according to grace" (Rom. 4:16). This formulation is highly compressed and lacks a subject or a verb, allowing a completion such as that suggested by C. K. Barrett: "God's plan was made to rest upon faith in order that it might be a matter of grace."[6] The emphasis is on "the promised inheritance which is achieved by faith and therefore by grace."[7]

At the climax of Abraham and Sarah's story, contrary to all human expectations, the miracle of grace occurred. Sarah conceived and bore a son from whom all the people of Israel ultimately were thought to have descended. And we Christians look back on that event just as Paul did, seeing our inclusion into the people of Abraham's promise as coming through faith as well. Paul felt that the promise came "not only to those of the law [the Jews] but also to those of the faith of Abraham, who is the father of us all [i.e., we Gentiles as well]" (Rom. 4:16). Paul perceived that this story reveals the hidden but universal structure of the new life in Christ enjoyed by Jews and Gentiles alike.[8] In Christ, the tender mercies of God were expressed to everyone on earth. He loved people without their

---

5. *2 Baruch* 57:2, cited by C. H. Dodd, *The Epistle of Paul to the Romans* (London: Hodder & Stoughton, 1932), p. 68.

6. C. K. Barrett, *A Commentary on the Epistle to the Romans* (New York: Harper & Row, 1957), pp. 95-96. See also C. E. B. Cranfield, *A Critical and Exegetical Commentary on the Epistle to the Romans* (Edinburgh: Clark, 1975), p. 242.

7. Ernst Käsemann, *Commentary on Romans,* trans. G. W. Bromiley (Grand Rapids: Eerdmans, 1980), p. 121.

8. Most commentators stress that the "all" in verse 16 includes

deserving it. Even when they killed him, Jesus said, "Abba, forgive them, for they know not what they do" (Luke 23:34). So for Paul, the death and resurrection of Christ offer us each a place in Abraham's promise. Since God's grace comes to us without our deserving it, we are all heirs of Abraham's promised future, recipients of the tender mercies of God that come when we have no reason to expect them. Paul presents this as the hidden plot of every human life.

One reason the film *Tender Mercies* rings true is that it follows this hidden plot. The film opens with a fight scene in a run-down motel room. Mac Sledge emerges from his drunken stupor two days later to face the bright sun "in the bleak west Texas landscape." The camera makes the "tiny gas station and motel" appear as "a fragile refuge in this wilderness," in the words of film reviewer Richard A. Blake.[9] Sledge admits that he has nothing to pay the bill: "Lady, I'm broke." The owner of the tiny motel and gas station, Rosa Lee, gives him work to pay off the bill. She cleans up his filthy room while he picks up debris and fixes screen doors.

Without any dialogue to explain what's on his mind, Sledge indicates that he would like to stay on. Rosa Lee offers him a room, meals, and $2 an hour in wages. They eat in silence at the end of a day's work, until Sunny, Rosa Lee's son, asks, "What's your name?"

"Mac" is the reply.

Jewish and Gentile Christians; for instance, Dodd speaks of the "universality of the Christian religion" at this point (*Romans,* p. 70). But Paul seems explicitly to go beyond such parameters to include persons of Jewish faith as well by the formulation "not only to those of the law." See Otto Michel, *Der Brief an die Römer* (Göttingen: Vandenhoeck & Ruprecht, 1978), p. 170; and Franz Mussner, "Wer ist 'der ganze Samen' in Röm 4,16?" in *Begegnung mit dem Wort: Festschrift für Heinrich Zimmermann,* ed. Joseph Zmijewski and Ernst Nellessen (Bonn: Hanstein, 1980); Bonner biblische Beiträge 53:213-17.

9. Richard A. Blake, "Texas Agape," *America,* 23 April 1983, p. 322.

Sunny asks the visitor, "Did you ever know my daddy?"
"No."
"Would you like him if you did know him?"
"Sure."
The next day all three drive to church, where Mac is seen
next to Sunny singing the hymn. After the service, the pastor
greets folks at the door of the church. Sunny says he wants to
be baptized, and the pastor asks Sledge when he was baptized.
Sledge says he wasn't. The pastor replies, "We'll have to work
on you then."

In subsequent scenes Mac and Rosa Lee begin to talk
about their families. Her husband was killed in Vietnam; her
father and mother died shortly thereafter. Mac says he has a
daughter, quite a bit older than her son. Sledge is next seen
working in the garden, and Rosa Lee appears. He asks her
whether she has ever thought about marrying again. She says
yes, she has thought about it. He asks her to think about
marrying him. She says, "I will think about it." In a later scene,
when a new country western group comes to meet Mac, he
introduces Rosa Lee as his wife. The gift of love happened
offstage, as it were. It is an undeserved grace, a gift of providence from a simple woman who continues to pray for him
and to be grateful for him. To quote the words of Richard
Blake again, "Mac does nothing to earn love and salvation;
these things simply come to him for no apparent reason, as
though salvation were his destiny."[10]

Although refusing to perform because his voice is so
worn out, Mac now begins to compose again. He revisits the
Oprey house where his former wife is performing. Her lyrics
deal with the old theme of cheap love: the "best part of all . . .
the room at the end of the hall, where everything's made all
right." She and her lover can "celebrate the heaven that we've
found" in the "best bedroom in town." Mac is seen in the

10. Ibid.

crowd while she sings about having tried so hard "to keep you off my mind . . . nothing's changed, and I'm still here for the taking." Refusing the allure of this false relationship, Sledge walks out. He returns home to face the loss of his own career, coming very close to betraying his commitment to avoid alcohol. The film allows us to overhear Rosa Lee's prayers during this dark time: "Show me thy way, O Lord, and lead me in thy truth. . . . For salvation do I wait on thee, all the day." (This prayer is an embodiment of the fidelity that stands at the center of Horton Foote's own life and work. Despite all the setbacks in his writing career, he told Samuel G. Freedman of the *New York Times* that his wife Lillian "kept me goin'. She never lost faith, and that's a rare thing. I don't know how we got through it, but we got through it.")[11]

The story of Mac Sledge's conversion, like most of the other important events in the film, takes place offstage. We see him in church, where Rosa Lee is singing in the choir, "Jesus, Savior, Pilot me." Sunny is baptized and the church sits in silence as Mac Sledge goes next. Someone says routinely, "Amen." As the family is driving home after church, Sunny says, "Well, we done it, Mac, we were baptized. Everybody said I was gonna feel like a changed person. I guess I do feel a little different but not a whole lot different. Do you?" Mac shakes his head. No lightning bolt has struck him thus far. Sunny says, "You don't look any different," and Mac smiles: "Not yet."

As Pauline Kael remarked, "Mac's conversion, like his falling in love, takes place off camera; that could be one of the mercies referred to in the title."[12] Precisely! But in contrast to Kael's skepticism, this is perfectly congruent with the theme of faith in the hidden mercies of God, the secret plot of the life of faith in Romans.

11. Samuel G. Freedman, "From the Heart of Texas," *New York Times Magazine,* 9 February 1986, p. 50.
12. Pauline Kael, "The Current Cinema," *The New Yorker,* 16 May 1983, p. 120.

The scene now shifts to a small dance hall a few days later where the new country western band is performing. Mac is singing the new song he has composed:

> If you just hold the ladder, I'll climb up.
> If you'll stand beside me all the way,
> I'll do all the things that didn't matter yesterday. . . .
> I'll be everything this man can be,
> If you just hold the ladder, baby, I'll climb to the top.

This expresses in country western language the plot of our text: grace — someone else holding the ladder — and faith — climbing up when it is available. The ultimate source of the ladder in Mac Sledge's life may be invisible and off camera to him as well as to us, but he senses that it is there and holds on tight to the future that has been given to him. To use Paul's words once again, "it is from faith, thus according to grace" (Rom. 4:16).

At the end of the film, having attended his daughter's funeral after she was senselessly killed in a car accident, Mac is picking up junk at the edge of the road near the house. Sunny comes home from school and asks his mother how his father was killed in Vietnam. She replies that it could have been a battle, or he could have been out walking. No one knows. Sunny goes outdoors with his football and runs toward Mac. They throw the ball back and forth while Rosa Lee looks on from the house. A new future is emerging between a stepfather and his son, slowly and unexpectedly in the midst of the mysteries of life and death. The message of this film is that we don't have any final assurances, any more than Abraham did. But we can respond in faith to the tender mercies we have received.

II

Paul describes the structure of these tender mercies in a way that is rather congruent with the film. He uses two succinct phrases in Romans 4:17 to describe the God of mercies, the One in whom Abraham had faith: God "gives life to the dead" and he "calls that which does not exist into being." While the concepts of resurrection and creation come from Paul's Jewish tradition,[13] his formulation suggests parallels to salvation by faith, to resurrection from the dead, and to creation from nothing.[14] As Ernst Käsemann explains, "creation, resurrection, and justification declare in fact one and the same divine action. This means that justification, as the restitution of creation and as resurrection anticipated in the stage of trial . . . , is the decisive motif of Paul's soteriology."[15]

Abraham was saved by faith, but God's gift to him of a future did not depend on his prior achievement or virtue. The promise was given to him as a sheer gift, unearned and undeserved. Paul perceived the same structure in the theme of resurrection. The God who "gives life to the dead"[16] provides a future for those who have lost everything, even life itself. The dead have no power to save themselves. Resurrection, the cen-

---

13. See the discussion in Michel, *Der Brief an die Römer,* p. 171, and Otfried Hofius, "Eine altjüdische Parallele zu Röm 4.17b," *New Testament Studies* 18 (1971-72): 93-94.

14. For an approach that questions this parallelism, see Klaus Berger, "Abraham in den paulinischen Hauptbriefen," *Münchener Theologische Zeitschrift* 17 (1966): 72.

15. Käsemann, *Commentary on Romans,* p. 123.

16. This phrase appears to be a direct quotation of the second benediction in the traditional Eighteen Benedictions prayer of Rabbinic Judaism, which in this context would pick up the theme of Abraham's aged body being "as good as dead" (Rom. 4:19). But the lifting up of this theme also expresses the central motif of Paul's Christian faith; it is as if the Abraham story were being viewed through the lens of Jesus' resurrection. See Cranfield, *Romans,* p. 244, and Ulrich Wilckens, *Der Brief an die Römer* (Zürich: Benzinger, 1978), 1:274.

tral theme of Easter faith, is God's miraculous intervention in behalf of those who are powerless, whose time is up. But Paul also finds this structure in the symbol of creation itself. God "calls that which does not exist into being."[17] The Creator God always makes something out of nothing, expressing transcendence over the created order and freedom from cultural manipulation.[18]

A structure of divine reversal thus stands at the heart of the Abrahamic faith in the mercies of God. Those who deserve no mercy receive it; those who are dead are offered new life; and that which is nothing is brought into existence. This structure lies at the heart of every authentic experience of tender mercies, including Horton Foote's own story.

That Mac Sledge does not deserve the mercies of God is honestly portrayed throughout the film. He is a profane, bitter, destructive person at the very end of his resources. One of the saddest scenes in the film is when his daughter Sue Ann comes to visit. Mac indicates that he had written letters over the years, but she says she never got them. Her mother had tried to cut off all relations with her destructive former husband. "I told Mama I was coming," Sue Ann confided. "She said she'd have me arrested if I did." Finally in this "awkward, hesitant, tentative" scene Sue Ann asks about the song he had sung to her when she was young, a song about the "wings of a white dove." Does he remember? Mac says, "No . . . maybe it was someone else."

Film critic Colin Westerbeck writes: "This exchange seems to be just the last of many missteps in their reunion, a

---

17. This is a characteristic idea in Hellenistic Judaism, visible in Philo, *Spec. Leg.* 4.187, *Op. Mund.* 81, and *Vit. Mos.* 2.100, as well as in *2 Baruch* 48:8. See Cranfield, *Romans*, p. 245.

18. See James D. G. Dunn, *Romans 1–8* (Dallas: Word, 1988), p. 237: "the individual or nation is dependent on the unconditional grace of God as much for covenant life as for created life. It was this total dependence on God for very existence itself which man forgot, his rejection of that dependence which lies at the root of his malaise (1:18-28)."

final and rather minor failure of memory to make up for absence."[19] But I think Horton Foote had something much more significant in mind. Here is a denial of a decent and tenderly caring aspect of Sledge's relationship to his daughter years ago. His singing had conveyed a sense of divine care that the child had needed and now yearns for again, far more than the fancy cars and big allowances that her mother is providing.

> On the wings of a snow white dove,
>   He came with his pure white love,
> With light from above,
>   On the wings of a dove.

Mac Sledge had conveyed God's tender mercy to his daughter without fully understanding it himself, and now he turns his back on it. Only when his daughter drives off — for the last time before her fatal automobile accident — does he return to the living room and hum the song he knows full well. It is a failure that he will never be able to redress.

This theme of personal, moral, and spiritual failure is closely linked with the death and resurrection theme in the film. That Sledge for all intents and purposes was dead at the beginning of the film is strongly suggested by the photography. His consciousness of the threat of death is also conveyed by curious details in the dialogue. When he can't sing one of the songs he has written because his voice is shot, he says with irritation, "Don't feel sorry for me, Rosa Lee, I'm not dead yet." Later he is asked by a fan of the new band that is playing his music, "Hey mister, were you really Mac Sledge?" He smiles and says, "I guess I was." But it is in reaction to the accident involving his daughter that Sledge confronts the reality and puzzle of death most directly. He tells Rosa Lee about how he deserved to die in place of his daughter:

19. Colin L. Westerbeck, Jr., "Unsung Heroes: Robert Duvall in 'Tender Mercies,'" *Commonweal* 118 (8 April 1983): 210.

> I was almost killed once in a car accident . . . I was drunk.
> They took me out of the car for dead, but I lived. I prayed
> last night to know why I lived and she died. But I got no
> answer to my prayer. I still don't know why she died and I
> lived. I don't know a blessed thing. I don't know why I
> came back to this part of Texas, and you took me in and
> straightened me out. Why, why did that happen? Is there a
> reason? And Sunny's daddy died in the war. My daughter
> killed in an automobile accident. Why? See, I don't trust
> happiness.

Mac Sledge can't trust happiness, but he does trust the
tender mercies that mysteriously led him from death to life. It
is also a leading from nothingness to existence, to use the words
of Romans 4:17. Sledge is depicted as having nothing at the
start of the story. He has lost his voice and his talent along
with his future. His career is gone. His family is gone. As a
schoolmate said tauntingly to Sunny on the playground, the
man staying at their home is nothing but a "silly drunk." And
yet mysteriously in the course of the film, Sledge begins to be
someone again. He gradually regains the use of his talents. As
one of the reviewers of the film remarked, Sledge "is, like the
legendary Phoenix, to rise from the ashes."[20] Although low-
key throughout, this story is just as miraculous as the creation
of something out of nothing celebrated by biblical writers.
Robert Hatch describes the filmmaker's intent: "Bent on cele-
brating the recuperative power of the human spirit, he leads
his hero into temptation but delivers him from evil, and the
audience I was in seemed dazed by the euphoria of witnessing
a miracle."[21] But unlike the usual miracles of film and television
fantasy, this one occurs mysteriously, off camera. That's what
dazes us. It is a matter of faith, elusive and intangible. All we

20. Blake, "Texas Agape," p. 322.
21. Robert Hatch, "Tender Mercies . . . ," *The Nation* 236 (30 April
1983): 554.

can witness is that a person who was once almost nothing becomes something at the end of the story, singing his own new songs and tossing a football to his newfound son.

III

The details of these stories of Abraham and Sarah, Mac and Rosa Lee may not match those of your life. But if you have ever experienced the tender mercies of God, the structure is probably the same. The God of tender mercies searches out the dead to make them alive, the nonexistent to bring them into being once again. It is mercy that gives us a future when we don't deserve it, when we have squandered it and thrown it away. But God's mercy appears most often beyond the range of the camera. God does not ordinarily come out into the open as in the film *O God,* in which he takes the form of a determined George Burns who performs public miracles to convince the world of his message. These two films, in fact, embody opposing strands in our religious heritage. In *O God* we find the pseudoscientific notion that God demonstrates his existence by performing miracles right in front of our eyes. When an automobile is filled with water on command right in the middle of the street on a dry day, the obviousness typical of fundamentalism is being claimed in the proof of God's existence and power. But Horton Foote's script is closer to the biblical truth. God's ways are too elusive[22] for our science, too far off the graph for objective proof. Yet the miracles of mercy are there for all who have faith to see.

So the final question is this: can we who are involved in the mysteries of healing gaze beneath the surface of our lives

---

22. For an exposition of this theme, see Samuel L. Terrien, *The Elusive Presence: Toward a New Biblical Theology* (San Francisco: Harper & Row, 1978).

to discern the hidden plot of tender mercies? Can we develop the skill and courage to follow the tiny clues that may lead to a viable future, despite all our failures and betrayals? The work of Horton Foote and the Apostle Paul urges us to hold fast to the mercies we have received, no matter how far offstage they may be occurring. We are called to set our faith in the God of tender mercies, to be faithful to the relationships through which those mercies are conveyed. Despite the necessity of scientific discipline in all of our fields, there is no need to turn our backs on the simple ways in which we convey God's "pure sweet love" to each other, "on the wings of a dove." For the God of tender mercies is the final source of any knowledge we may have of the mystery of life. The God of Abraham and Sarah and Paul is the one "who gives life to the dead, and calls that which does not exist into being."

Life's Unlimited Value
and Our Limited Resources

Jim Wallis

Where there is no vision, the people perish.

— Proverbs 29:18, KJV

THERE IS AN OLD SLOGAN from the civil rights movement that
goes like this: "The differences between us stem from what we
see when we get out of bed in the morning." Theologians
would call that contextual theology. It's true.

As I approach this critical topic, "Life's Unlimited Value
and Our Limited Resources," I can't get away from what I see
when I get out of bed every morning in my own neighborhood.
The most critical question concerning the value of life and how
much we value it is all right there before my eyes. At the heart
of the question is a very common phrase that has become quite
acceptable to us — the phrase "us and them."

My neighborhood of Columbia Heights in Washington,
D.C., runs along 14th Street, a scene of the much-publicized,
so-called riots following the assassination of Martin Luther
King, Jr., in the bitter spring of 1968. The now infamous "riot
corridor," as the area is still called, even today bears the scars

15

of the frustrated and angry violence that erupted when people's hopes were suddenly and brutally cut down.

Several years ago, my sister Barbara was walking through the neighborhood with her five-year-old son Michael. They were on their way to the Sojourners day-care center. Michael surveyed the scene on the block and, looking up at his mother with puzzlement, asked, "Mommy, was there a war here?"

Perhaps the eyes of a child can see what jaded adult vision quickly passes over or too easily accepts — there was and is a war here. It goes on every day, and the casualties are everywhere.

The people who inhabit this and similar neighborhoods are not only neglected and ignored by political decision makers; they are war victims. They are the dead and wounded of a system that has ravaged their lives and their communities. It is no wonder that those who make it through refer to themselves as "survivors." But many are not surviving. The forces that have declared war on them are global and impersonal, but the consequences for the people here are very personal indeed.

For most of the fourteen years Sojourners Community has lived in Washington, D.C., the inner-city neighborhoods of the capital have been invisible to the nation. Everyone knows "official Washington" with its marble, monuments, and malls. But "the other Washington" has been off-limits to the blue-and-white tour buses and to the consciousness of the rest of the country.

Even the name "Washington, D.C." tells the tale of two cities. The white residents and professionals who run the federal capital live in "Washington." The black residents who are the city's vast majority (70 percent) are from "D.C." — the District of Columbia. This capital of the "free world" is still virtually a segregated city, especially in housing, schools, and social interchange.

A word heard often in D.C. is "colony." The District of Columbia didn't obtain even partial home rule until 1974. Even today, District residents (700,000 people) have no voting representation in Congress, and all actions taken by the elected city government are subject to congressional veto.

The forces of housing gentrification and real estate speculation are slowly pushing black residents into more over-crowded neighborhoods or out of the city altogether. Once-poor ghetto neighborhoods are being transformed into upscale yuppie enclaves, with prices too high for any of their former inhabitants.

Neither the extremes of wealth and poverty in Washington, D.C., nor its racial polarization have been well known beyond the "beltway," the highway encircling the metropolitan area.

But recently Washington, D.C., suddenly began to make national and international headlines — not as the center of power but as the "murder capital" of the nation. Quickly the media cameras so used to turning away from "the other Washington" focused their attention on neighborhoods overrun with drugs and guns. D.C. got famous. *Newsweek* did cover stories that spoke of the "two Washingtons," while nervous local officials rushed to assure anxious tourists that the killing was limited only to "certain parts of the city."

Vincent Harding, an author and historian of the civil rights movement, recently made a trip to West Germany, where he led retreats for black American soldiers. Many told Harding that they were re-enlisting in the army so that they could keep from going home to their own neighborhoods, where they were afraid of being killed. Young African-Americans were deciding to stay in the army to save their lives.

We are losing a whole generation of young people in our cities to poverty, drugs, and violence. Washington, D.C., is a city out of control, reeling from the brutal consequences and tremendous suffering of a global economic, social, and spiritual crisis that has yet to be named, understood, or addressed. It is a crisis of the highest magnitude, and it points to a global reality that we must recognize and squarely face.

Through these painful and soul-searching events, something has become quite clear to me: Washington, D.C., stands now as a parable unto the world. The crisis in the capital of the wealthiest and most powerful nation in the world tells the story of the crisis the whole world now faces. In Washington, D.C., today, we see a mirror of what the global system has become.

Washington, D.C., is literally a symbol of power. People stream to the official city to exercise power, to influence power, or just to be around power. The power holders and the power groupies alike are intoxicated with the smell of it. The key word here is *access*. Access to power — that's what everyone is always fighting for in this town. Power, like money, becomes its own justification. How you get it and what it's used for are beside the point; having power is what's important.

If Washington is the most powerful city in the nation, D.C. is the most powerless, without control even over its own affairs and destiny. As the "Last Colony," D.C. symbolizes the relationship many other parts of the world have with official Washington. The revealing paradoxes exist on almost every level of life in Washington, D.C. Housing costs are among the highest in the country, as are the rates of the homeless. Infant mortality is at Third-World levels in a city that contains more lawyers and real estate developers than any other. Black youth unemployment is above sixty percent, while white professional couples with two incomes search for investments. Scholastic Aptitude Test scores for students in D.C.'s public schools are one hundred points below the national average, while students in the city's private schools score one hundred points above it.

Washington, D.C., is a microcosm of the dynamics that now govern the world order. The current drug war brings all of these contradictions into sharp relief. No one knows the exact numbers, but an extraordinary percentage of D.C. youth are involved in the drug traffic. As in source countries such as Colombia, drug trafficking has become a livelihood for the poor. In the high-stakes atmosphere of drugs and money, life becomes cheap indeed. In Colombia, it now costs only forty dollars to have someone murdered. In both Colombia and Washington, D.C., poverty sets the stage for tragedy, and the drama of drugs simply carries out the executions.

In the current economic and cultural environment, it becomes very difficult to tell young people "Just say no to drugs." What we are in effect telling them is to be content working part-time at McDonald's (the eighth largest employer in D.C.) and pursuing the American Dream as best they can. In a changing economy, the better jobs and brighter future we want to promise inner-city children are just not there.

Meanwhile, the images that assault them daily — through television, movies, and popular music — all tell young people that their very worth and status as human beings come from how much they can possess and consume. Fancy clothes, new cars, a nice house, and lots of gold around their necks become the aspirations of inner-city youth. In that, they are no different from most Americans. The crucial difference is that these inner-city youth are virtually denied legal access to the alluring attractions of American consumer culture. They are blocked out by an economy that has no room for them.

Whole sectors of the global population are now simply defined outside of the economic mainstream. And to be shut out of the global economy means to be consigned to death. Like Jesus' parable of the rich man and the beggar Lazarus, millions and millions of God's children are now shut outside the gate of the global economy.

More and more children live in poverty in America. One out of every five children, and half of all black children, are born poor. The gap between rich and poor has steadily grown as a changing economy leaves more and more people behind. The swelling ranks of the hungry and homeless, now including many families, are a highly visible moral contradiction in a nation that prides itself on its standard of living.

The earth itself suffers along with the poor. Our politically neglected and continually poisoned environment faces real threats from global warming trends, ozone depletion, acid rain, contaminated water, unhealthful food, polluted air, toxic and nuclear wastes, and ravaged wildlife. We will not escape the consequences of our behavior. As Native American leader Chief Seattle said years ago, "This we know. The earth does not belong to people. People belong to the earth. This we know. All things are connected. Whatever befalls the earth befalls the people of the earth. We did not weave the web of life. We are but a mere strand in it. Whatever we do to the web, we do to ourselves!"

In the United States, public school education, health care, low-cost housing, the family farm, and the industrial workplace are all in a state of crisis. Crime is out of control, while the proposed solutions fail to deal adequately with either underlying causes or individual responsibility, neglecting both perpetrators and victims.

The fight against racism has been halted at the highest levels of government, and its ugly resurgence is upon us. Hard-won progress made by women for equal rights is now under attack from many quarters. The nation's foreign policy continues to violate its expressed values and causes untold human suffering, principally among poor people of color.

Things are especially hard on the black and brown minority youth that inhabit our inner cities. They are the ones whose dreams and hopes for the future have been denied. There is no room for them in this society, and they know it. With no place, no stake, and no future available to them, they are finding their own road to "success." And it is a very dangerous road indeed, with many casualties strewn along the way. On this road, young people can make more money in a day or a week than they ever dreamed possible. Thousands of dollars are available to them in an economy that has never offered them more than uncertain, part-time employment at minimum wage. And many are taking the option.

In a series of articles called "At the Roots of the Violence," *The Washington Post* described the unwritten "code of conduct" of the drug dealers in their own words: "Never back down . . . be willing to kill or die to defend your honor. . . . Protect your reputation and manhood at all cost." The drug dealers who live by this code are known on the street as "soldiers." A reporter asked one of them why they are always so ready to shoot. "I guess it's greed for that money," was his answer. The *Post* then commented on the code of the streets: "it is a way of behaving that flies in the face of traditional American values."

Is that really true? What values are reflected in American foreign policy? What code of ethics governs the wars of Wall Street? Do not the enshrinement of greed and the glorification of violence every day on TV sets and movie screens reinforce cultural values? With great danger to themselves and others, are not these children of the poor pursuing the same glittering materialistic dream of others, in the quickest and perhaps the only way they see open to them?

Drugs are not the only narcotic here. Addiction to the money that comes from drugs is what is leading to the violence. That addiction — the addiction to materialism — is fed every hour of every day in this society. It is not only legal to feed that addiction; it is the whole purpose of the system. It is our reason for being as a people — to possess and consume.

The images dance before us every waking moment. The images attract, lure, and create desire; they awaken the greed and covetousness of our worst selves. Our children are glued to the TV screen; the beat of incessant consumption pounds in their ears. Shopping malls have become the temples, shrines, and communal centers of modern America.

The issue here is deeper than greed and selfishness. Material consumption — buying and using things — has become the only means left of belonging in America. If we can't buy, if we can't consume, we simply don't belong.

The violent underside of American society is not a social aberration that we can safely and morally distance from "traditional American values." Rather, the frightening carnage is a frustrated mirror image of the twisted values that now govern the wider society.

We should know by now that we can't have an economic system that leaves masses of people behind without ensuring endless conflict. We should know by now that we can't have security based on weapons and technology that lead us to being participants in a mutual suicide pact. We should know by now that growth and progress that abuse, exploit, and destroy our natural environment will end up choking us to death. We should know by now that we cannot deny human dignity to our neighbor because of race or class or sex without destroying our own soul. The logic of the system is literally killing us.

A New Vision

Any new vision for the future will have to challenge fundamentally the system at its roots and offer genuine alternatives based on the critical moral values that we still possess. Two crucial constituencies for such a task are the poor themselves and those places within the religious community where fresh thinking and renewal are now taking place. The future will not be constructed from the mere shuffling of elite personnel at the top; rather, it will be a response to a transformation of values and action at the grassroots.

Despite the lack of recognition of this fact, we are indeed in a social crisis. It is a crisis that confronts us with choices — critical choices of national values and direction. Honest truth-telling and bold moral vision for the future are urgently needed. The combination of the two is in fact the essence of what political leadership must be in the days ahead.

A discernible hunger exists in the nation for just such

leadership. Whether it is strong enough to produce a winning electoral possibility in the near future is a question we can't answer yet. But the American people deserve to be offered such a choice. And, even more important, we have a religious responsibility to offer it. That has always been the prophetic vocation.

The biblical prophets challenged the way things were, while at the same time helping people to imagine new possibilities. They were not afraid to confront the king, to defend the poor, or to say that what God had in mind was far different from what most people had settled for. Rankled by injustice, sickened by violence, and outraged by oppression, the prophets defined true religion as "to act justly and to love mercy and to walk humbly with your God" (Micah 6:8, NIV).

Our political convictions must grow out of that kind of faith — a faith that does justice. We should be less interested in the ideologies of Left and Right than in whether justice is really being done — especially to the marginalized and downtrodden for whom the God of the Bible seems to have such a special concern. That same biblical perspective sees the accumulation of wealth and weapons as the wrong road to national security. Instead it offers the possibility of an economy that has room for everyone, an environment treated as a sacred trust, and a commitment to resolving our conflicts in ways that do not threaten the very survival of the planet.

That political vision directly confronts the barriers of race, class, and sex that so violate God's creative purpose and still wreak such violence among us. To enjoy a culture in which human values and creativity can truly flourish will mean being set free from our captivity to consumption and its totally economic definition of life. What is most human rather than what is most profitable must become the critical question.

A few years ago at a press conference of the Reagan White House, then–Attorney General Edwin Meese declared to the nation that there are no hungry people in America. The next day was Saturday, and, as usual, food lines formed early outside the Sojourners Neighborhood Center, only one and a half miles from the White House. Three hundred families receive a bag of groceries each Saturday that is critical for getting through the week. Just before the doors are opened, all of those who helped to prepare and sort the food join hands to pray.

The prayer is normally offered by Mrs. Mary Glover, a sixty-year-old black woman who knows what it is to be poor and who knows how to pray. She prays like someone who knows to whom she is talking. You can tell that Mary Glover has been praying to her God for a long time.

She thanks God for the gift of another day. Then she prays, "Lord, we know that you'll be coming through this line today, so help us to treat you well." Mrs. Glover knows very well who it is that waits in line with the hungry and huddles with the homeless to keep warm on the steam grates of Washington, D.C.

She knows the meaning of Jesus' words in Matthew 25 where he says, "I was hungry and you gave me no food, I was thirsty and you gave me no drink, I was a stranger and you did not welcome me, naked and you did not clothe me, sick and in prison and you did not visit me" (vv. 42-43).

And Mrs. Glover gives the people's response: "Lord, when did we see you hungry and thirsty and naked, a stranger, sick, and imprisoned? We didn't know it was you. Had we known it was you, we would have done something. We would have responded. Had we just known it was you, we would have at least formed a Social Action Committee. But we didn't know it was you!"

And Jesus responds, "As you have done it to the least of these, you have done it to me." To those who would name his name, Jesus asks, "How much do you love me? I'll know how much you love me by how you love them."

Mary Glover understands Matthew 25. Her prayer is the best commentary on these verses from the Gospel of Matthew that I've ever heard.

Perhaps an image of God for us in our times is a black grandmother in the inner city weeping and mourning the loss of her children — a whole generation of young people who are simply being abandoned and destroyed. If we become angry — with all of our sin, complicity, and limited compassion — how angry must God be at what's happening?

The most pressing issue today is that we really have no sense of solidarity with one another — no communion, no community, no common bond. And what is happening in my neighborhood is a very telling example. In my neighborhood, and throughout the country, a whole generation of young people is being destroyed. But for most Americans, this is just an inner-city problem, a crime concern, a drug crisis, or a violence issue. What is really happening is that a whole generation of us is being destroyed — but white America doesn't see it that way. It isn't "us." It's "them." How can we call people who are desperately poor and struggling to survive a "permanent underclass"?

In the slums of Manila, I saw whole families washing plastic and styrofoam they had picked up off the streets to sell for a living. At the end of the day you can make two dollars if you wash enough plastic. They are us, and we are them. And we are deeply connected.

If we fail to see these connections, we are simply not going to make it. All of our other problems stem from this one. At the heart of all of these issues is a single issue — that we have lost our sense of being brothers and sisters, daughters and sons of God. We are the children of God, and we are inextricably bound to one another. Either we will live together, or we will die as those who have forgotten that they are part of a common destiny.

Jesus has addressed the basic spiritual problem we face — a lack of human solidarity with one another — by taking on the identity and flesh of the ones we have abandoned and saying, "What you have done to the least of these, you have

done to me." This was and is God's way of teaching us the
human solidarity we must learn in order to survive and fulfill
our creative purpose — God literally becomes the one we've
decided is unimportant.

Matthew 25:31-46 provides the crucial insight and con-
verting word we need in order to re-establish our lost solidarity with one another. It is as clear a word as can be found about
the judgment of God upon the ways in which we are treating
one another and about the command of God to change our
ways. This is no abstract judgment; Christ himself assumes the
form and flesh of our many victims and cries out to us to stop.
"You are not just killing them," exclaims Jesus, "you are killing
me!"

It is time to heed the words of the prophet Amos: "But
let justice roll on like a river, righteousness like a never-failing
stream!" (5:24, NIV). "Let justice roll" into the streets of oppression and drugs and hopelessness, and also into the avenues
of luxury and fear. "Let justice roll" into the ghettos and
barrios and squatter camps, but also into the affluent suburbs
of comfort and indifference. "Let justice roll" into the board-
rooms of corporate wealth and the corridors of political power.
"Let justice roll" into a church made lukewarm by its confor-
mity and isolated by its lack of compassion. "Let justice roll"
and set free all the captives — those under bondage to
poverty's chains and those under bondage to money's desires.
"Let justice roll" — and let faith come alive again in all of those
whose eyes long to see a new day.

Most U.S. political leaders are drawing all the wrong
lessons from the tumultuous happenings in the Eastern bloc.
They see these events as vindication rather than as prophecy.
"Communism has failed and we have won!" they proudly
exclaim. That perspective is as shortsighted as it is self-serving,
for history will overtake the West as well. It's only a matter of
time. Here, too, the system is failing while we struggle to keep
up the illusions. Our inner cities, which have become war

zones, are but the first sign of a global economy that is unraveling.

The historic events we witness today are prophetic. Today an east wind of freedom and democracy is blowing out the old. Tomorrow a south wind of justice and liberation will blow to set free the oppressed. You cannot cheer democracy for Polish workers, Lithuanian farmers, and Chinese students while you block freedom from South African laborers, Salvadoran *campesinos,* and Korean slum dwellers. When the south wind blows with the hopes of the world's poor on its wings, it will cause a chilly gale to be felt by those northern global power centers that run the world's system of economic apartheid.

Today an ugly wall of ideological repression is tumbling down. Tomorrow the invisible walls of international trade, finance, and economic oppression will also come tumbling down.

It's hard to stop the wind when it begins to blow.

Life and Peace:
Antidote to Violence

Roy I. Sano

MANY DIFFERENT ISSUES spring to mind when we think of violence. Perhaps the most obvious issue of violence is the threat of armed conflict among and within nation states.[1] Surely the rising levels of violent crimes on America's streets will come to mind, as well as domestic violence within American society — spouse abuse, child abuse, and violence directed against the elderly. We may also think of the abuse of our natural environment, whether in mining or in agriculture, in leisure activities or in the disposal of wastes. These and many other issues come to mind when we think of violence, and all cry out for attention.

As a member of an ethnic minority, however, I have chosen to direct our thinking to the issue of racial violence, and to offer racial harmony as an antidote to the persisting

1. See *In Defense of Creation: The Nuclear Crisis and a Just Peace* (Nashville: Graded Press, 1986), a pastoral letter issued by the United Methodist Council of Bishops, of which I am a member. Much of this document remains relevant even in the post–cold war era. Both superpowers continue to develop thermonuclear and biochemical weapons and participate in "low-level conflicts" that could escalate.

violence in the human family. While I support the ecumenical concern of the World Council of Churches regarding "global racism," the council's broader and more overarching approach must not divert our attention from the domestic issues of racism closer to home.

I will begin by analyzing violence in race relations. While the type of data cited may be familiar, a few features of the analytical framework may be sufficiently novel to warrant reintroduction here.[2] The analysis will explain the relevance of our inherited "foundational concepts and doctrines which support our faith in human life as a loan from God who endows us with freedom to live responsibly within the limited conditions of nature, society, and culture." These foundational ideas, images, and symbols provide "theological and pastoral in-

2. I outlined an analytical framework for racism in *From Every Nation Without Number: Racial and Ethnic Diversity in United Methodism* (Nashville: Cokesbury, 1982). The approach follows most closely the one summarized earlier in Harry H. L. Kitano and Roger Daniels, *American Racism: Exploration of the Nature of Prejudice* (Englewood Cliffs, N.J.: Prentice-Hall, 1970), and developed succinctly and applied broadly by Kitano in *Race Relations*, 3rd ed. (Englewood Cliffs, N.J.: Prentice-Hall, 1985). While he acknowledges a variety of patterns in ethnic relations, Kitano focuses on internal colonialism as the primary source of our most serious problems.

The concept of "internal colonialism" also appears, for example, in Albert Memmi's *The Colonizer and the Colonized* (Boston: Beacon Press, 1965), and in Robert Blauner's *Racial Oppression in America* (New York: Harper & Row, 1972). The stratification and domination that are central to the concept of colonialism is crucial in Joe R. Feagin and Clairece Booher Feagin, *Discrimination American Style: Institutional Racism and Sexism* (Englewood Cliffs, N.J.: Prentice-Hall, 1978); Joe R. Feagin, *Racial and Ethnic Relations* (Englewood Cliffs, N.J.: Prentice-Hall, 1978); and Reid Luhman and Stuart Gilman, *Race and Ethnic Relations: The Social and Political Experience of Minority Groups* (Belmont, Calif.: Wadsworth, 1980).

Alternative readings of race relations appear, for example, in Thomas Sowell's *Ethnic America: A History* (New York: Basic Books, 1981), and are listed in Kitano, *Race Relations*, pp. 22-23, 44-45, 63-64, and 80-81.

sights, interpretations, and motivations for ministry by chaplains, parish clergy, and laity."[3]

Violence in Race Relations

Individual Dimensions of Racism

Acts of violence based on race are again on the rise in this society. According to a 1987 study conducted by the Center for Democratic Renewal in Atlanta, Georgia, "Not a day has passed in the last seven years without someone in the United States being victimized by hate violence."[4]

One such incident will illustrate the importance of these phenomena. In 1988, Jack Purdy went on his murderous rampage in Stockton, California, killing five Southeast Asian children on a school playground. At first the reports suggested that it was an act of a deranged man. Investigations later revealed his festering hatred toward racial minorities in general, and his particular hostility toward Vietnamese people.

The consequences of this single incident still run deep. Several adults can hardly bring themselves to go shopping for fear of the risks entailed in leaving their homes. One grandfather, immobilized by terror, must be forcibly lifted from his bed to eat at the dinner table. Children still suffer physical symptoms from the trauma of seeing schoolmates gunned down before their eyes.

A comment by David H. Bennett in this connection is somewhat troubling. In his otherwise useful book, *The Party*

3. *In Defense of Creation.*
4. Chris Lutz, *They Don't All Wear Sheets: A Chronology of Racist and Far Right Violence — 1980-86* (New York: Division of Church and Society, National Council of the Churches of Christ in the U.S.A., 1987), p. 11.

of Fear, the professor of history at Syracuse University offers an incisive historical survey of nativist movements and an illuminating study of "the new right" in our society. He describes the development and activities of such white identity and hate groups as the Silent Brotherhood, the Posse Comitatus, the Aryan Nations Churches, and the CSA (the Covenant, the Sword, and the Arm of the Lord). Bennett observes:

> No real movement arose on the neo-Nazi Right, merely the fantasies and frustrations of a poorly educated group of outsiders, some with criminal records. They lived in areas far removed from the urban centers of power, angry loners from the mountainous Northwest, the Ozarks, and the upper Midwest. These racist sects provided a way of dealing with their anger and their fears. It is an old tradition in America, if now a stunted one.[5]

While these sects may remain stunted in their membership and far removed from population centers, one act of violence by such individuals sends shock waves reverberating through segments of our population. We cannot overlook the significance of these individual acts.

This insightful observation made by Stokely Carmichael and Charles V. Hamilton in 1967 remains true today:

> When white terrorists bomb a black church and kill five black children, that is an act of *individual racism,* widely deplored by most segments of the society. But when in that same city — Birmingham, Alabama — black babies die each year because of the lack of proper food, shelter, and medical facilities, and thousands more are destroyed and maimed physically, emotionally, and intellectually because of condi-

---

5. David H. Bennett, *The Party of Fear: From Nativist Movements to the New Right in American History* (Chapel Hill: University of North Carolina Press, 1988), p. 356.

tions of poverty and discrimination in the black community, that is a function of *institutional racism.*[6]

We must turn, therefore, from the individual expressions of racial violence to the violence perpetrated by systems in this society.

Institutional Dimensions of Racism

The institutional dimensions of racism in this society are evident in a closely linked series of factors: residence largely determines educational experiences, educational experiences largely determine employment patterns, and employment patterns largely determine the income level. In addition to the crucial role played by these four basic factors of residence, education, employment, and income, there are other factors and indicators of the institutional manifestations of racism. Key among these are participation in politics or decision-making organizations, inclusion in financial institutions, treatment in the criminal justice system, accessibility to health-care services, and expressions in various cultural outlets. These additional factors and indicators perpetuate patterns found in the four basic factors of residence and education, employment and income.

Imagine these four basic factors as closely linked sections of two circular tracks, tracks on which persons move through two distinct cycles. For persons of light color, and particularly whites, the factors in their circle create something like an es-

6. Stokely Carmichael and Charles V. Hamilton, *Black Power: The Politics of Liberation in America* (New York: Vintage Books, 1967), p. 4. (Emphasis added.) The concept of "institutional racism" was popularized in a landmark volume entitled *Institutional Racism in America*, ed. Louis L. Knowles and Kenneth Prewitt (Englewood Cliffs, N.J.: Prentice-Hall, 1979). This collective effort studied the expressions of racism in the economy, public schools, administration of justice, health delivery systems, residential patterns, and general ethos in the United States.

calator spiraling ever onward and upward. The factors in the other circular track generally move blacks, Hispanics, American Indians, and large segments of Asian and Pacific peoples round and round on the same plane or downward, with the circle becoming smaller and more crowded at every turn.

Then imagine if you will that a larger circle surrounds the circle on which people of color move. The additional factors in that larger circle confine those persons within that small and crowded circle and add momentum to their movement through the same basic experiences in housing, education, employment, and income. So long as people of color are confined to this chain of factors and its adverse impacts, we perpetuate and deepen the exploitation, oppression, and violence committed against them.

We seldom recognize the enormity of the task when we try to counteract the violence committed by any one of those factors or propose to break persons loose from those tightly linked circles. In most cases, each of the factors has a built-in dynamism and a backup system. Consider education: the pattern of disadvantage experienced in elementary grade levels is only compounded by disparities experienced in intermediate and high school grade levels. Even if mounting efforts may have succeeded in graduating increasing numbers of blacks and Hispanics from high school during the 1980s, their enrollment in colleges and universities slipped seriously during the same period because the discrimination and segregation experienced at that level with even greater effect demanded more than their resources could surmount.

In 1988, twenty years after the publication of the historic Kerner Report, a conference was held to review efforts to curb the adverse effects of the factors cited above and to break the linkages between them. The Commission on the Cities, together with the University of New Mexico Institute for Public Policy and the Johnson Foundation in Dallas, Texas, staged this national conference to study the updated analysis.

Fred Harris and Roger W. Wilkins wrote the following in the introduction to a collection of studies presented at the conference:

> For a time after the Kerner Report, and through the mid-1970s, we made progress on all fronts. Then came a series of economic shocks: recessions, manufacturing moves and closings, the flight of jobs and the middle class to the suburbs, and a reduction in real wages. These blows hit the most vulnerable Americans the hardest. There were determined efforts to cut social programs in education, housing, jobs, training, and other areas. The Reagan administration was hostile to affirmative action and to vigorous enforcement of the civil-rights laws.[7]

In answer to the question "What is the present situation on race and poverty in the United States?" they wrote:

> The Kerner Report is coming true: America is again becoming two societies, one black (and, today, we can add to that Hispanic),[8] one white — separate and unequal. . . . There are "quiet riots" in all of America's central cities: unemployment, poverty, social disorganization, segregation, family disintegration, housing and school deterioration, and crime are worse now. These "quiet riots" are not as alarming as the violent riots of twenty years ago, or as noticeable to outsiders. But they are even more destructive of human life. National security requires renewed human investment if we are to be a stable and secure society of self-esteem. We have the means. We must summon the will.[9]

7. Fred R. Harris and Roger W. Wilkins, eds., *Quiet Riots: Race and Poverty in the U.S., The Kerner Report Twenty Years Later* (New York: Pantheon Books, 1988), p. xii.

8. Surely one must also add American Indians and segments of Asian and Pacific peoples in the United States.

9. Harris and Wilkins, *Quiet Riots,* pp. xii-xiii.

If we bear in mind the impact of these experiences upon society as a whole and the toll they are taking on us individually and in our neighborhoods, we might be likely to agree with Harry Kitano's observation: "The central problem of our era is that of the relationship between different colors and cultures."[10] But if we agree with this claim, why does it not grab our attention and mobilize us into action? Several reasons come to mind. One is fatigue. The energy and dedication, the thought and care invested in earlier efforts to rectify the situation have left many of us exhausted, discouraged, and despairing.

Another reason, however, is ideological. The issue of race remains a subordinate concern and it is difficult to mobilize action against racism. I must therefore turn to consider the ideological dimensions of racism that explain the lower priority given to averting violence in race relations.

Ideological Dimensions of Racism

Many discussions of racism turn rather quickly to a definition of racism. They describe, for example, the prejudicial attitudes and discriminatory actions that segregate persons of color to a lower status in society. They acknowledge informal patterns of action in social arrangements as well as more formally adopted policies and established patterns. Such descriptions of racism will also proceed to suggest that the sense of racial superiority among whites and a condescending feeling toward racial and ethnic minorities lie behind the racist attitudes, actions, social arrangements, and established policies.

The rationale behind these attitudes, actions, arrangements, and policies is often treated as the ideological dimension of racism. There are also subtler ideological dimensions of racism which make it very difficult to muster our energy for

10. Kitano, *Race Relations*, p. 8.

sustained action against violence in race relations, and which hamper us in our efforts to mobilize our professions, churches, and political parties into action.

In his book entitled *Racial Oppression in America*,[11] Robert Blauner describes the low ranking of race relations in our prioritized list of issues. Blauner says that the subordinate status given to ethnic relations is shaped largely by several key modes of perceiving social reality that we have imported from Europe. These analytical models for social experiences describe the cultural heritage of white Americans whose ancestral roots are in Europe. That is to say, they describe the transition from rural to urban societies, from agricultural economy to industrialization, following the work of such sociologists as Tönnies, Marx, and Weber.

These analytical models suggest that the identifiable ethnic diversity among people was superseded by a relatively homogeneous population in premodern times. The implication is that in modern times ethnic identity and relations are no longer pressing issues. The racist consequences of this perception and assumption become evident in Blauner's thesis. The efforts of racial and ethnic minorities in this society to preserve and cultivate their distinct identities are regarded as premodern, antiquated concerns for the benighted. Ethnic issues become non-issues.

We learned years ago from that classic in American literature by Ralph Ellison, *Invisible Man*,[12] that racism makes people of color disappear from the consciousness and perceptions of others. I am saying that there is a racist consequence to those erudite insights of authoritative interpreters of our social experiences. They provide the ideological grounds for dismissing racial issues, and they explain people's impatience

11. Robert Blauner, *Racial Oppression in America* (New York: Harper & Row, 1972), pp. 12-13.
12. Ralph Ellison, *Invisible Man* (New York: New American Library, 1947).

with them. It is difficult to take seriously issues that are not supposed to exist. People have little patience with those who say that racially distinct people still exist when they were supposed to have disappeared long ago. The clash between the assumption of their disappearance and the mounting reality of their presence creates resistance and stress in this society.

What is true of the social sciences is equally true of behavioral sciences. This is particularly evident in psychology, which is also the most influential of the auxiliary disciplines in the practice of ministry in the United States today. Various schools of psychology proceed with an easy assumption that we are working with a homogeneous population, and thus a single model of the human psyche is considered sufficient. The subtle nuances in the psychodynamics of racially and ethnically diverse people are invisible to us because the analytical models which determine our perceptions do not take them into account. Hence the neglect of racial dimensions in our diagnoses of illnesses, in our therapeutic practices, and in our counseling or pastoral ministry.

As ministers, whether lay or ordained, we are called to address racism in all its dimensions — individual, institutional, and ideological. While no one of us could possibly address the full range of issues, analyzing racism within this broad framework may help us to understand it better and may motivate us to work together to promote life and peace.

Promoting Life and Peace

What, then, is the meaning of life and peace as an antidote to violence in race relations? In examining this question we will be following the main tenets of trinitarian theology, the foundational concepts and doctrines that shape Christian ministry, lay and ordained. I will be speaking from a Protestant perspective, and with appreciation for the Jewish roots that inform my ministry.[13]

Salvation and the Savior

I begin with salvation and the Savior because in the Protestant tradition that is the primary focus of much of our efforts to promote *shalom* — wholeness, health, and peace — as an antidote to the violence described earlier. A passage from the Apostle Paul summarizes several key qualities in *shalom:*

> Therefore, since we are justified by faith, we have peace with God through our Lord Jesus Christ. Through him we have obtained access to this grace in which we stand, and we rejoice in our hope of sharing the glory of God. More than that, we rejoice in our sufferings, knowing that suffering produces endurance, and endurance produces character, and character produces hope, and hope does not disappoint us, because God's love has been poured into our hearts through the Holy Spirit which has been given to us. (Rom. 5:1-5)

The passage refers to three key moments in salvation. First is *justification,* which entails "peace with God through our Lord Jesus Christ." The second is the change in a person that brings rejoicing in suffering along with endurance, character, hope, and love; by tradition, we describe such change as *sanctification.* Third, Paul speaks of "sharing the glory of God," referring to the *perfection* or fulfillment yet to come. I will say more about this in relation to the Sanctifier.

13. While I as an Asian American have grown increasingly aware of the ways in which Buddhism, Taoism, Confucianism, and Shintoism have informed my Christian faith and calling, this is not the time or setting to trace their possible contributions to the practice of Christian ministry.

For now we will concentrate on the first two — justification and sanctification.

Reconciliation

Whatever psychological, social, political, or economic improvement we seek, if we overlook these key moments of salvation we lose one of the most basic contributions Christians can offer in ministry. Justification and sanctification, peace with God and transformation of persons — and all despite suffering — are among the most fundamental dimensions of life and peace that act as antidotes to violence in race relations.

I speak as one who received opportunities to turn a hand-me-down religion in a warm Christian family into a personally experienced faith at a crucial point in my life. During the disruptions and turmoil of World War II, courageous Christians came to say good-bye to a despised people when we Japanese-Americans left our homes for America's version of a "concentration camp" out in Arizona. The same kind of courageous and caring Christians came to live and work among us in those camps. Others set us captives free by offering employment for my father and housing for our family in Pennsylvania. In a strange land, far across the continent, still other Christians took us in. Little wonder then that as a lad of sixteen I walked forward to kneel at an altar during a camp meeting in Pennsylvania. Because of the courageous witness and costly caring of Christians, I chose to trust that island of acceptance I found in a turbulent ocean of wartime hysteria and hate that could have engulfed me.

The night I knelt at the altar I experienced an overwhelming release from dreadful burdens of fear and rejection I did not even know I carried. Changes began to occur inside me. Healing of wounds grew stronger.

As the years passed I came to see what was behind those kind gestures of Christians. I found an explanation in such words as those in Romans 5:1-5. Those caring Christians had experienced peace with God through a Savior, whose life set in motion an antidote to the violence committed against us. This antidote curbed and counteracted the painful violations of human dignity committed by individuals, the death threats from the awesome institutions of the military and intelligence agencies, and the tidal wave of racism in those frightful days in the 1940s.

If we Christians do not create settings where people can experience peace with God and release from hurts and burdens through the healing we have through Christ, we are failing to offer a very basic contribution that ministry in Christ should provide.

My conversion illustrates the role of *reconciliation* in the salvation offered in Christ. Reconciliation is usually applied narrowly to justification or forgiveness of sin. I am using the concept more broadly to include justification and sanctification, as Paul does in Romans 5. While "peace with God" refers most immediately to justification, it is also related to our transformation or sanctification into the likeness of God's strength, truth, life, and love.

Redemption, Reunion, and Restoration

In addition to the reconciliation or healing that I experienced because of the courageous and caring witness of Christians, three other ingredients of my salvation and redemption also came through the gracious love and care of Christians. I will refer to these ingredients or stages as redemption, reunion, and restoration.

Quakers, members of the Society of Friends, contributed two ingredients. They offered my dad employment and our family a home. The offer made it possible for us to leave the camp in Poston, Arizona, and gave us an opportunity to start a new life in Pennsylvania. Release from incarceration illustrates what I mean by *redemption*. In biblical language we might speak of deliverance; in contemporary parlance we are likely to speak of liberation. The offer of employment and housing depicts something of what I mean by *restoration*.

When we settled in Media, Pennsylvania, we began attending what was then the First Methodist Church. The congregation took us in, thanks to the leadership of the pastor, Chester Buzzard, his wife Hazel, and key laypersons. This welcome into a predominantly white congregation and into friendships at school illustrates what I mean by *reunion*. All three ingredients — redemption, reunion, and restoration — were integral to my salvation.

In the inherited ordering of doctrines, most Protestant theologies restrict salvation to reconciliation — which includes justification, sanctification, and perfection — and say that redemption, reunion, and restoration are merely preparations for, or by-products of, salvation as reconciliation; they are not, strictly speaking, part of salvation. This view is understandable. The orthodox Protestant theology restricts salvation to justification and sanctification. The Wesleyans, or Methodists, add perfection. As a matter of fact, we even have a Latin phrase for salvation understood in these terms, thus insuring a sacrosanct status to the doctrine. The *ordo salutis* (order of salvation), as it is called, includes these three steps: justification, sanctification, and perfection.

Because the hallowed moments of salvation are restricted to the steps in the *ordo salutis*, efforts and experiences associated with redemption, reunion, and restoration are relegated to secular status. Release of captives from prison (redemption), reuniting them with the broader community (reunion), and rebuilding the natural and social environment to provide the basic necessities of life (restoration) are made to appear secular if divine work in general and salvation in particular are limited to the *ordo salutis*. Ventures and ministries associated with redemption, reunion, and restoration are categorized as political or economic interests, or social and cultural pursuits, but not as a part of salvation in the strict sense of the word.

I agreed with this approach until I began reflecting on my involvement during the late sixties in the struggles for justice among racial minorities. I also started dealing with my sexism through a divorce, and participated in opposition to neocolonialism in the Vietnam war. Participation in these movements and events had a hallowing quality that counteracted the violations of human dignity contained in each of these issues. Involvement in these efforts recovered some measure of sanctity in the face of sacrileges suffered. To use a biblical and theological term, we encountered a holiness. For us Christians, we encountered the Holy One unrelenting in restoring wholeness, life, and health in the face of sin and death. Praises be to this God of the Hebrew Scriptures and the New Covenant community!

Reflections on these experiences and on other analogous experiences among persons of color at home and abroad have uncovered biblical models for a new ordering of the doctrines related to salvation. In Ezekiel 36, for example, we find the story of Exodus restated for the Babylonian captives, with the promise of a new Exodus, a new covenant, and a return to the promised land. The "new covenant" Ezekiel promises to the captives was described earlier by Jeremiah (see Jer. 31:33-34). It has three steps or ingredients. First, there is pardon or justification, depicted here as washing: "I will sprinkle clean water upon you, and you shall be clean from all your uncleannesses" (Ezek. 36:25). Second, there is renewal of God's image through sanctification; God's people will receive a new heart and a new spirit: "A new heart I will give you, and a new spirit I will put within you; and I will take out of your flesh the heart of stone and give you a heart of flesh" (36:26). Third, they will become an obedient people, suggestive of perfection: "And I will put my spirit within you, and cause you to walk in my statutes and be careful to observe my ordinances" (36:27). The result of these steps is reconciliation: "You shall be my people, and I will be your God" (36:28). This is the same sequence of steps found in the *ordo salutis,* moving from justification, through sanctification, to perfection, and thus achieving reconciliation.

But Ezekiel is announcing something more here. The experience of salvation as reconciliation occurs within a broader *history of salvation.* In the verses just preceding this passage, Yahweh makes three additional promises: "I will *take* you from the nations, and *gather* you from all the countries, and *bring* you into your own land" (36:24, emphasis added). These three additional acts of taking, gathering, and bringing announce to the captives in Babylon that God is staging a new Exodus, offering them a new covenant, and bringing them back to their own land, their own liveable space. "Taking," "gathering," and "bringing" here depict what I have called redemption, reunion, and restoration.

Two additional points are related to this broader view of salvation. First, the holiness of God is established by his actions: "It is not for your sake, O house of Israel, that I am about to act, but for the sake of my holy name" (36:22). That is, the holiness of God is established through the justification, sanctification, and perfection in reconciliation, as well as through redemption, reunion, and restoration. What we call the "history of salvation" is not secular history. The social, economic, and political dimensions of liberation struggles, as well as efforts to promote harmony in race relations and create liveable space, should not distract us from the wholeness of the Holy One of Israel at work. These apparently secular efforts are also part of a holy history, the "history of salvation" or *Heilsgeschichte,* as German scholars have called it. And rightly so, because redemption, reunion, and restoration are as much a part of salvation as the justification, sanctification, and perfection that lead to reconciliation.

The second observation related to this broader view of salvation is that Yahweh promises an evangelistic outcome through the twofold stories of the history of salvation and the *ordo salutis:*

> The nations will know that I am the Lord [Yahweh as Sovereign and Savior], says the Lord God, when through you I vindicate my holiness before their eyes. (Ezek. 36:23b)

Any full ministry that seeks to promote wholeness of life, *shalom,* or peace will create opportunities for victims of racial violence to experience reconciliation through the traditional steps of the *ordo salutis.* Furthermore, we will also join God in releasing the captives and setting free the oppressed (redemption). We will join Christ in breaking down "the dividing walls of hostility" (Eph. 2:14) and gathering diverse people in community (reunion). And finally, we will join the God of the Garden of Eden, the God of the Exodus, the God who delivered captives from Babylon, the God who liberated early Christians from Roman domination, in creating liveable space as a setting for meaningful work and leisure (restoration).

Creation and Consummation

The traditional emphasis in Protestantism on transformation through salvation needs balancing today. If we are always stressing change — even desirable change — to the exclusion of affirming what exists, we run the danger of doing further violence to people. Balancing the work of the Christ with the work of the Creator and the Consummator will promote an appreciation for the fullness of the life God intends for us.

The issue of balancing salvation with creation and consummation emerged early in the Christian community in the debate concerning circumcision. Should Gentile Christians undergo circumcision when they joined the new covenant community? The biblical injunction calling for circumcision for the covenant people of God made it appear obvious which way early Christians should go (see, e.g., Gen. 17:10-14). But they chose otherwise, and for even better biblical reasons. For members of the early church, who were predominantly Jewish, God is one. The work of God as Savior therefore could not contradict the work of God as Creator or as Consummator. Thus, Gentiles should be allowed to be Gentiles just as God had created them; and in the consummation, Gentiles will still be recognizable Gentiles, just as Jews will remain recognizable Jews (Rev. 7:1-12; 21:9-14).

These references to Gentiles and Jews offer instructive clues for the next steps in race relations. The treatment of Gentiles in the early church has provided familiar lessons concerning racial minorities. Although debatable on several points, the main thrust of our ministry is to affirm and celebrate the distinct identities of racial minorities. We do not demand that they circumcise themselves of the unique qualities that the Creator God has cultivated through time. While the mounting resistance to pluralism remains, I seriously doubt if it can ultimately bury the affirmation of racial, ethnic, and cultural diversity in the Christian household of faith.

But what are the contemporary implications of the early church's assertion that Jews can remain Jews, the bearers of God's earlier revelations? The point has bearing with regard to certain efforts to address white racism among Caucasians. In their zeal for helping racial minorities, some white persons have been known to try to become racial minorities themselves. This is often accompanied by something approaching self-hatred because they are white. We can understand this. The burden of guilt was laid upon the heads of whites when the Kerner Report said concerning racism: "White institutions created it, white institutions maintained it, and white society condoned it."[14]

Some years ago, John Howard Griffin symbolized such efforts to become a racial minority. "He took injections to

14. *Report of the National Advisory Commission on Civil Disorder* (New York: Bantam Books, 1968), p. 2.

darken his skin, subjected himself to hours under a sun lamp, shaved his straight hair, and emerged on the streets of New Orleans a black man."[15] James T. Baker's incisive criticism of Griffin reminds us that he had earlier assumed the role of a Frenchman when studying abroad, an aborigine when living in the South Pacific, an undercover agent in Mexico, and even a Trappist monk like Thomas Merton. While Baker acknowledges our great debt to Griffin's *Black Like Me* (1961), he raises serious questions about the authenticity of its witness. Baker points out that Griffin could finally never become a black person, partly because the "grease paint," as he called it, would fade. Besides, in his imitations of the black experience, he remained who he was. In reporting on a visit with Griffin, Baker says,

> Griffin embraced me. It was a Texas embrace. And when he said good-bye, it was with a decided drawl. I knew, as perhaps only a fellow Texan could know, that this man who was recognized in the world as a sophisticated, cosmopolitan Catholic . . . who had cast his lot (temporarily) with oppressed southern blacks . . . was at heart a small-town boy from the hardscrabble farmlands of red-neck central Texas.

Baker observed how he "despised his own ethnic origins":

> in playing his roles he consistently denied the culture that was inherently his own and thereby missed a grand opportunity to speak prophetically to it from the inside. His was a world, like it or not, of southwestern white Protestantism, liberally laced with moonshine whiskey and country music. By insistently stepping out of it — to be Francophonic, to be Catholic, to be black, to be a hermit — he accomplished minor triumphs by missing the greater opportunity to live the Christian life amid the sounds of twangy low-church preaching and western swing.

15. James T. Baker, "John Howard Griffin: Christian in Grease Paint," *The Christian Century,* 22-29 December 1982, p. 1313. My analysis of Griffin follows this article.

We may find Baker's demands excessively restrictive if he is asking Griffin to remain in the narrow confines of his Southwestern Protestant heritage in a small town in Texas. But the call for Griffin to affirm his own identity, calling him back to his roots, rather than spending his whole life being someone else, is surely needed today. We have some scary expressions of white self-affirmation from the religious and political right. More options are needed.

In drawing this essay to a close, I would remind you of two persons who acknowledge and affirm their distinct white Protestant roots and yet participate in a wide range of interaction. The first is Will D. Campbell, in his book *Brother to a Dragonfly* and later in his *Forty Acres and a Goat: A Memoir*.[16] As a Baptist preacher in Mississippi and Tennessee, Campbell has taken a leading role in the civil rights movement, working freely among black and white people for justice and reconciliation. The second is Garrison Keillor in his *Lake Wobegon Days,* a collection of his well-loved stories of the little town of Lake Wobegon, a town where the "good old days" are still alive and well.[17] Keillor explains why we cannot find Lake Wobegon. When surveyors went through that part of the country to check the earlier measurements, they discovered a mistake. After they redrew the lines, Lake Wobegon disappeared from the map.

Keillor speaks for those who know their place on the map has been in some measure a mistake. They sense they are pushed off the map and cannot return to that place in the past they have known. And yet, he goes on ruminating.

We follow him to this particular place many of us knew, even if we are not from the Midwest, reliving with him the fun and foibles, the meanness and majesty of a day we carry with us. In the meantime, we have undergone changes. Keillor

16. Will D. Campbell, *Brother to a Dragonfly* (New York: Seabury Press, 1979); *Forty Acres and a Goat: A Memoir* (San Francisco: Harper & Row, 1986).

17. Garrison Keillor, *Lake Wobegon Days* (New York: Viking-Penguin, 1985).

depicts the changes well when he says of Lake Wobegon, "The women are strong, the men are good-looking, and all the children are above average." Those who follow Keillor in his stories are those who have moved with the shifting values and social arrangements for women and men, where we are not on top of the heap but are finding ways to live with change and memories, dignity and humor, hurts and hopes.

What I see in Campbell and Keillor is something that is most crucial for racial minorities in our struggles: an affirmation of identity balanced with a celebration of the changes that can heal us. If you ask me why I became a Christian and answered God's call to service, it was because I heard the inner witness of the Spirit: Let them call you what they will, but hear this, "You are a child of God!" (see Rom. 8:16). I heard that word through Christians and then, through them, from God's very self.

We usually associate that witness with the experiences of salvation, but I would point out that the same word of affirmation is present in the story of creation. God looked upon creation and "saw that it was good . . . very good" (Gen. 1:4, 10, 18, 25, 31). Under the providence of God creatures undergo changes, and these evolving identities can also be celebrated.

People of color at home and abroad have said to whites, particularly white males, "You are a curse on humankind, the scourge of the earth." I invite you to listen to the witness of the Spirit: Let them call you what they will, but hear this, "You are a child of God." In the vision of the consummation there is a place for Jews as well as those "from every nation, from all tribes and peoples and tongues" (Rev. 7:9). Hallelujah!

The Christian doctrines that report the work of God as Creator, Christ, and Consummator provide the foundations for promoting life and peace as an antidote to the violence in this world. Praises be to God!

Food, the Basis of Life:
An Appeal to Eliminate Hunger

Robert F. Drinan, S.J.

THE WORLD HAS BEEN transformed by the explosions of moral energy in the U.S.S.R., in Eastern Europe, and in South Africa that began in 1989. I have become persuaded that, however important and intractable the domestic problems in the United States may appear, they cannot be compared in significance with the new global challenges that confront the United States and indeed the whole world.

The global opportunities now facing the United States are possibly even greater and more awesome than the world situation at the end of World War II. At that time, the nation somehow rose to the leadership of a ravaged world. It radiated a moral vision that made the attainment of peace and the realization of human rights the principal objectives of the global village.

The United States was the principal mover in establishing the United Nations and its subsidiary organs, all designed to prevent another world war. International entities were created, such as the World Health Organization, the Food and Agricultural Organization, the World Bank, and the International Monetary Fund. This moral vision was also evidenced by the establishment of the Peace Corps, the enactment of Public Law 480, the Food for Peace Program, and the initiation of several programs to bring food to underdeveloped nations.

During the forty years of the cold war, Americans instinctively knew that they stood as a beacon light of hope for the people of the world. One could say, in fact, that two hundred years of American democracy have given the entire world a set of moral ideals that have been the inspiration of peoples everywhere. Those ideals originally came, of course, from England and the common law; they were not the invention of America. But they are now the basis of the law and the heart of the aspirations of people in English-speaking nations and almost everywhere on the globe.

But from the outset of the postwar years, attempts to achieve those ideals have faced severe setbacks. Soon after the war, the U.S.S.R. occupied several nations in Eastern Europe. In 1949 it formed an alliance with mainline Communist China and startled the United States by its aggressive colonialism in the Third World. The United States sought to respond by developing and carrying out a plan to contain communism. History will have to judge whether that policy was wise or foolish, but it is now a part of the past. America's motivations gradually became mixed and confused. It clearly deviated from its vision of peace and justice with its unilateral overtures into regional wars and its partial abdication of the ideals and objectives of the United Nations and its specialized agencies. In the 1970s and thereafter, the energies and the enthusiasms behind world humanitarian programs declined. The cynicism engendered by Vietnam and Watergate helped to bring about the so-called "me generation" of the 1970s and 1980s.

It is almost impossible to overstate the significance of what happened in 1989: the coexistence in terror between the superpowers came to an end; some 300 million persons in the Soviet Union and Eastern Europe are voting for the first time in two generations; and the 28 million black people of South

Africa now seem to be on the road to some form of a desegregated and democratic society. But in spite of these significant events, the problems confronting America in 1945 were clear and simple compared to those which must be faced in the 1990s.

We must recognize an entirely new world that is no longer immobilized by the fear of communism — if it ever was — but is suffering from widespread malnutrition, growing illiteracy, and a ravaged and poisoned environment.

We must face the consequences of the undeniable probability that the world's population will increase from 5.1 billion in 1990 to 6.2 in the year 2000. The advent of 1.1 billion new humans in ten years is even more awesome than the economic collapse of Europe and the bankruptcy of Japan in 1945.

We must also recognize that in the 1990s the estimated number of malnourished persons — now 800 million — may well increase, and that the needless deaths of children from starvation — now thousands per day — could continue to grow. The number of persons who are illiterate, now in the one billion range, may also rise as a hindrance to economic development.

Adding to the urgency of all of this is the possibility that these millions of persons who have been deprived of their basic economic rights may well rise up and demand social justice like the millions who in 1989 demanded and received their political rights. In Africa, millions of black citizens, living in the world's poorest societies, may be inspired by the example of the people of South Africa to rise up and obtain some form of equality.

The world has changed so radically that the priorities of the United States simply must be modified at least, or even substantially altered. There is no war on communism to use up America's energy. And we are gradually realizing that America's absorption in that crusade against communism has left the United States economically impaired and even very vulnerable to its economic rivals.

Undoubtedly, many Americans will refuse to see the new crises in the world. Isolated by two oceans and insulated from the world by the highest standard of living in the history of the universe, Americans forget that they make up less than five percent of the world's population and that their history and destiny are to serve as a moral model to the world.

The United States has never abolished the dream that it created for the world in the Nuremberg Trials, the United Nations Charter, and the Marshall Plan. The people of America can take not a little satisfaction in the realization that it was America's ideals which inspired the people of Eastern Europe in 1989 to demand that they be given the right of self-determination.

The United States is able and indeed is morally required to ponder and act on the unbelievable array of opportunities presented to it; they are imperiously calling for action. Surely the massive expenditures on arms engaged in by both superpowers and by other nations — $900 billion in 1989 — can be constructively channeled toward more noble objectives.

Few, if any, obligations challenge contemporary American leadership in the world arena as does the crucial proposition that every person should have adequate food. I shall describe four converging aspects of that challenge.

I. The Present Plight of the World's Hungry

One of the fundamental reasons why every eighth human being is malnourished is the vast diversion of money to arms that has taken place over the past two generations. In the years from 1947 to 1987, the United States spent $7.6 trillion on arms and armaments. It is simply unbelievable that the United States doubled its military budget during the 1980s — from $150 billion in 1980 to $300 billion in 1990.

Even if the sums expended for arms decrease sharply,

there is no certainty that the United States and other developed nations will join in a common program to assist the masses of people who, in countries that were once colonized by predominantly Christian nations, suffer intensely from hunger, disease, and illiteracy.

Willy Brandt spoke eloquently about the indifference, even the carelessness, of the rich nations in these words:

> History has taught us that wars produce hunger but we are less aware that mass poverty can lead to war or end in chaos. Where hunger rules, peace cannot prevail. He who wants to ban war must also ban mass poverty. Morally, it makes no difference whether a human being is killed in war or is condemned to starve to death because of the indifference of others.

The world scene is grim. Every sixty seconds, twenty-eight people die needlessly of hunger-related causes; nearly two thousand will thus die in the next hour. Two hundred and eighty thousand people die of starvation each week, or nearly 15 million per year.

One child in ten dies before its first birthday. In Latin America every fifth person is severely malnourished. Indeed, there are more hungry people proportionately in Latin America than in India, Pakistan, or Bangladesh. All of this is made more complex and tragic by the debt contracted by Latin America since 1975. Efforts to pay the service charges on these debts that total over $400 billion result in further dislocation of the economies of Latin America.

The lack of food is clearly correctable. Between 1950 and 1980, the world's population increased by 76 percent, but world food production rose by 124 percent. For the first time in the history of the world the problems of famine, pestilence, and drought are known to be solvable. Despite that hope, the World Bank recently predicted that in the year 2000 some 470 million people will still be living in absolute poverty — a condition defined as totally lacking in the basic elements essential to human dignity.

The years of the cold war were not a total loss for the war on hunger. Since 1960, forty-one nations have ended mass hunger within their borders, China being the most dramatic case. In addition, during the last several decades UNICEF and the World Health Organization have eradicated smallpox in the entire world — a plague that had claimed some twenty million victims a year. UNICEF is also working aggressively and effectively to eliminate the six major childhood diseases — measles, polio, tuberculosis, diphtheria, tetanus, and whooping cough. These diseases still, however, kill three million children a year — especially where children have little resistance to the diseases because of their malnourished state. Yet it can be demonstrated that with even a modest increase in funding, the lives of fifty million children — five million a year — could be saved during the 1990s.

II. Public Efforts to Guarantee the Right to Food

In 1945 all the nations that then belonged to the U.N. pledged hopefully in Article 55 of the Charter "to provide the highest standards of living, full employment . . . and conditions of economic and social progress and development."

On December 10, 1948, Article 25 of the Universal Declaration of Human Rights declared, for the first time in human history, that everyone has "the right to a standard of living adequate for the health and well-being of himself and his family, *including food*" (emphasis added).

That proclamation received legal embodiment in Article 11 of the United Nations Covenant on Economic Rights, which recognizes "the right of everyone . . . to . . . adequate food, clothing and housing." The signatory nations of that covenant — now numbering over one hundred — made specific pledges to "take appropriate steps to ensure the realization" of those rights.

In 1974 the United Nations issued the Declaration on the Eradication of Hunger, proclaiming that "every man, woman and child has the inalienable right to be free from hunger and malnutrition."

There is, therefore, an internationally recognized right to food. Consequently, all nations have formally accepted an obligation to make it possible for their own citizens to exercise this right. There is also a moral obligation on the part of international society to assist poorer nations in their quest for economic security.

Notable pledges have been made in the United States as well. In the 1950s Congress enacted the program "Food for Peace." President Kennedy pledged in 1961 that the United States would do two things in the 1960s: go to the moon, and provide that no child would go to bed hungry. Man landed on the moon in 1969. But how many children since then have died for lack of food?

The same promise about food was made in 1974, when President Ford, under intense pressure from the Congress, pledged to the Food and Agricultural Organization meeting in Rome that within a decade no child would go hungry. Nearly two decades later the situation is significantly worse.

In 1975, the U.S. Congress enacted a resolution that states that the right to food should be considered in the formulation of every decision about foreign policy.

Research on the right to food was done by the Presidential Commission on Hunger appointed by President Carter in 1980 and chaired by Sol Linowitz, former ambassador to the Organization of American States. The commission urged the United States "to make the elimination of hunger the primary focus of its relationship with the developing nations." This objective is even more compelling, the commission added, since "it is possible to eliminate the worst aspects of hunger and malnutrition by the year 2000." The commission expressed the conviction that an effective campaign against world hunger "holds the key to global and national security." It added a pragmatic note, suggesting that an emphasis on the right to food would help U.S. farmers by making available millions of acres now deliberately kept out of production by U.S. farm policy.

In 1980, in his first encyclical, Pope John Paul II emphasized that the areas of misery and hunger on our globe could have been made fertile in a short time if the gigantic investments in armaments had been changed into investments in the service of life.

Unfortunately there was no reference at all by the White House in the 1980s to the findings or the recommendations of the Presidential Commission on Hunger. But its conclusions are even more compelling in the 1990s.

No account of the public position of the United States on the right to food would be complete without mentioning the singular work of the late Congressman Mickey Leland of Houston. His untimely death in Ethiopia, while on a mission to bring food to that country, will not end but rather will reinvigorate the work of Congress's committee on world hunger which Congressman Leland established and chaired.

The United States has never refused to aid the international agencies designed to combat hunger, but the alleged or assumed generosity on the part of the United States cannot be verified in fact; the United States now ranks proportionately only fifteenth out of the seventeen nations that give aid to underdeveloped nations.

One has to conclude that the efforts of the United States to alleviate hunger have been spasmodic, episodic, and fragmented. We respond in faltering steps despite our memory that some 52 million immigrants came to American shores, very often impelled by the quest for food; millions fled the potato famine in Ireland, and many more fled from hunger in most of the nations of Europe. The United States is a nation made up of people who fled hunger or famine. Can the now-affluent citizens of America turn their backs on some 800 million persons who have hunger as their daily companion?

The lessons of the revolutions of 1989 are numerous. But one can hope that the people of America, the children of revolutionaries, will rise up against their own government when necessary and insist that it comply with both its obligations under international law and its own aspirations to ease starvation in the world.

Pope John Paul II asked the key piercing question on January 29, 1990. Arriving in the poor country of Burkina Faso — formerly Upper Volta — he asked the world: "How will history judge a generation that, having all the means to feed the world population, refused to do so?" John Paul continued: "In the name of Justice, the successor of Peter begs his brothers and sisters around the world not to scorn the hungry of this continent. . . ."

III. Private Initiatives Related to Hunger

Nongovernmental organizations devoted to internationally recognized human rights have surged in number and activity since the United Nations made human rights a central part of international law. At San Francisco in 1945, several such organizations helped to make human rights a crucial part of the Charter of the United Nations. And since the United States Congress and President Carter made human rights a core part of America's foreign policy, the number of U.S.-based human rights groups has multiplied.

These public interest groups have for the most part concentrated on political rather than economic rights. Amnesty International, established in 1961, deliberately and resolutely keeps its agenda on political rights. Now that political rights will be more available in large areas of the world, one can hope that some of the energy and enthusiasm of nongovernmental organizations devoted to political rights can be transferred to the struggle for economic rights.

These groups have been very effective at the mobilization of shame that was so clearly an element in the moral uprisings in 1989. Can we hope that the spiritual forces that brought people to the streets of Leipzig, Budapest, East Berlin, Prague, and Cape Town will now prompt millions of parents to rise up with their demands for food and medicine and books for their children?

A public interest group unique in America is the Christian-motivated, sixty thousand member group called Bread for the World. The founder, a Lutheran pastor named Arthur Simon, was the architect and the principal lobbyist for Congress' creation of a food grain reserve in the United States. Bread for the World has sensitized the United States to the urgent moral need of making it possible for millions to exercise their right to food. One has to think that if all religious groups in America worked for the objectives of Bread for the World, the foreign policy of this nation would change. This is especially true in the world after the cold war.

One also has to hope that the enormous energies of the peace movement will be redirected into efforts to ensure the right to food, now that the number one threat to public health, the nuclear threat, has been somewhat reduced with the end of the cold war. One such talented group within the peace movement is Physicians for Social Responsibility. These activists, who helped to end the Vietnam War and who have worked against the threats of the nuclear era, now have a new and important role.

A thousand new issues will emerge as the cold war fades away. Environmental issues such as global warming, destruction of the ozone layer, the disappearance of the rain forests, and the pollution of the world's rivers will continue to cry out for attention. Still, with so many millions of lives at stake, it can be argued persuasively that the right to food must take precedence in everyone's moral theology and in every citizen's approach to the public morality of America.

Perhaps the time has come for all of the churches and synagogues of America to come together for a Conference on Religion and the Right to Food. I recall the unprecedented interreligious Conference on Religion and Race in Chicago in 1963. An ecumenical gathering of 1,200 church-related officials issued a declaration on racism that was very influential in the enactment of the Civil Rights Act of 1964 and the Voting Rights Act of 1965.

During the years of the cold war, religious groups operated according to consensus positions on issues like civil rights, aid to the poor, and the need for a better immigration policy. They were less united on issues related to the containment of communism. It now seems realistic to hope that with the end of the cold war against communism, religious groups in America will come to have total solidarity and will employ this new togetherness to join in a war against global hunger.

IV. The Responsibilities of Individual Americans

As one looks at religious groups in the United States, the potential of the Catholic community is a striking example. The fifty-four million American Catholics are among the best-educated groups in the United States. They are upwardly mobile and they conduct an amazing array of Catholic schools, enrolling some three million students. American Catholics also maintain an extensive array of hospitals and an impressive number of social welfare agencies. In the twenty-five years since Vatican II, American Catholics have become intellectual, dynamic, articulate, and aggressive. Their bishops have promulgated pastorals on nuclear war and on the economy that have won praise for their pronouncements and also for the way in which those pronouncements were reached.

There are deep differences between religious groups in America, but on the issue of food for the world the faith community is powerfully united. The divine Word, in both Old and New Testaments, demands feeding the hungry. There is no issue that unites religionists and secularists more than that of global malnutrition. A new moment for interreligious collaboration has arrived in America. Everything is in place for the United States to assume a new and magnificent role.

The problem of global hunger is enormous. It is not simply a matter of bringing food to children. It also requires the formation of sound economic structures so that nations will be able to feed themselves. But the difficulties must not deter us from confronting the fact that we will be deemed enemies of God and humankind if we do nothing to stop the avoidable death of thousands of children each day.

Christians and others must learn, pray, and act. All three of these inseparably linked activities are essential for any resolution of the problem of world hunger. Any solution, furthermore, will in all probability come not from the Congress but from the people — and very possibly from the pews.

Americans have felt good because of the moral energy and the righteous indignation that were seen on display at Johannesburg, Warsaw, and Tiananmen Square. Indeed, we are taken aback at the suddenness of the collapse of the melancholy world of communism that we assumed drearily would be with us until we died. But abruptly and amazingly we are presented — by world history and by God's providence — with startling opportunities about which we had never even dreamed.

Not a few Americans feel overwhelmed by it all. They should remember the words of Margaret Mead: "Never doubt that a small group of thoughtful, committed citizens can change the world. Indeed, it is the only thing that ever has."

Americans must recall the deep moral heritage that is

theirs. George Santayana expressed it well: "Being American is in and of itself almost a moral condition." The moral mission of America can be summed up in these striking words of Archibald MacLeish:

> There are those who will say that the liberation of humanity, the freedom of man and mind are nothing but a dream. They are right. It is a dream. It is the American dream.

The Impact of Genetic Science on Theology

J. Robert Nelson

Scientific Technology as Context of Theology

ONE OF TODAY'S approved and popular adjectives modifying the word *theology* is *contextual*. To do theological thinking in its right context means to emancipate it from libraries and academic classrooms. It means that theology should arise from the "real-world" situations of poverty, oppression, racism, politics, and secular culture in general. The various theologies of liberation, as well as older conventional theologies, are thus defined by their appropriate contexts.

While we appreciate and appropriate the new challenges and hopes of contextual and liberation theologians, their warnings and promises have to be examined carefully to discern whether or not they are authentically Christian. Seldom noticed is the widespread blindness of many contextual theologians to the fact that one of the most prominent and important

Portions of this chapter were previously published in *Genetics and Law III*, ed. George Annas and Aubrey Milunsky (New York: Plenum, 1985), and used by permission.

contexts of human living today is that of science-based technology. Science and the technology springing from it are pervasive in societies and cultures everywhere on earth. They affect our ways of living at virtually every moment. They give us comfort and prosperity. But they also create many social problems and arouse much anxiety about the proximate and ultimate future of humanity. In an especially urgent way, recent research and techniques of genetic science are creating major theological tasks that Christian thinkers have scarcely begun to assume.

Relative to the numbers of practicing theologians, only a handful of persons are seriously engaged in relating the range of scientific research and achievement to religious beliefs and theological ethics. Of these, the majority seem to be more concerned with physics than with the biological sciences. Among the notable theologians concerned with the physical sciences are Stanley L. Jaki and Thomas F. Torrance — both recipients of the Templeton Award — Ian Barbour, William Pollard, Wolfhart Pannenberg, Günter Altner, and the circle that produces the journal *Zygon*. Those working on biological issues, which would seem to come much closer to human experience than physics, are A. R. Peacocke, John Habgood (the Archbishop of York), Charles Birch, James Childress, Philip Hefner, Roger Shinn, James Gustafson, Hans Schwarz, and Elving Anderson.

The very paucity of their numbers in contrast to the immensity of issues raised by physics and biology constitutes a challenge to younger theologians today. Theological students with excellent college education in the sciences are needed, as are persons who have become theological students later in life after having been research scientists and engineers. It is these persons especially who are equipped to undertake this urgent theological task. Others with less scientific knowledge but strong incentive to learn about science can also qualify for this avocation.

Dialectical Interaction and
the Method of Correlation

As for the true relation between science and religion, a dialectical interaction seems to be the best designation. All talk about estrangement and mutual hostility, as in the old cliché, "warfare between science and religion," is completely outmoded. Equally suspect is the easy, unambiguous notion of a synthesis of religion and science.[1] Just as the body of Christian faith and doctrine has its own integrity, the body of scientific knowledge and technological application also has an integrity of its own. Yet they must affect each other by mutual penetration of insights and understanding about the created order and human life. This is what is meant by their dialectical interaction.

The appropriate method of dealing critically with both dimensions in their mutual relation is that of *correlation*. The late Paul Tillich's wisdom on this method is compelling. As Tillich explained it, this method "tries to correlate the questions implied in the situation with the answers implied in the message."[2] The word *situation* here refers to virtually any event or process in human experience that stimulates our questioning; *message* refers to the given core of Christian faith — the gospel — and the great reservoir of historical interpretation and understanding of the gospel. However, this message is not considered to be a body of propositional or dogmatic statements containing all the right answers to every hypothetical scientific or ethical question.

The cluster of ethical questions that have been engendered by the rapidly expanding science of genetics provides a timely test of the method of correlation, which points to an

1. For criticism of an easy synthesis of religion and science, see James M. Gustafson, *Ethics from a Theocentric Perspective,* vol. 1 (Chicago: University of Chicago Press, 1981), pp. 353-54.

2. Paul Tillich, *Systematic Theology,* vol. 1 (Chicago: University of Chicago Press, 1951), p. 60.

effectual median between two unsatisfactory alternatives. One is the simple, mechanical deduction of ethical rules from allegedly eternal and revealed truths. The "hard lines" of both traditional Roman Catholicism and Protestant Biblicism meet and coincide by this method. Insofar as they conceive creation to be static and finished, both revere nature as absolute and immutable: "As it was in the beginning, is now and ever shall be." But what is "it" in this doxology? If "it" is creation as such, or human life within creation, then any tampering, manipulating, or modifying is sinful and prohibited. For some, this means no blood transfusions or surgical invasion; for others, no deviation from normal intercourse for procreation, no contraception, and no modification of genes in human tissue.[3]

The opposite of these hard lines are the theologically "soft lines" of prudential, utilitarian thinking. According to this way of thinking, any application of genetic or medical technology is acceptable, as long as beneficial or pleasurable results appear to outweigh painful or harmful results to individuals or classes of persons. Since American society is rapidly becoming very diverse in many ways, especially with respect to religious and moral pluralism, advocates of the soft line daintily avoid any taint of authoritarian judgment in the name of the God whom Christians worship. The hard line is called *deontology,* a word that emphasizes moral obligation to God; the soft line is called *libertarianism,* a word that stresses freedom from limitations. Is there an alternative between these two extremes?

Yes, correlation is such an alternative. It is not a simple, one-way approach from the questioning situation to the answering message; such would be merely a correlation by de-

3. The Vatican's "hard line" is made explicit in *Instruction on Respect for Human Life in Its Origin and on the Dignity of Procreation,* Congregation for the Doctrine of the Faith, 1987.

duction. Instead, there is reciprocity between situation and message, or (to use Tillich's words) between "human existence and divine manifestation." Correlation is a dialectical method. It presupposes an interaction between situation and message, between genetics and Genesis, between DNA and divinity.

We say, quite easily, that Christian faith expresses our "ultimate concern," which is God's purpose for life. But genetic science likewise deals with a matter of ultimate concern to all of us living mortals — namely, human life as such. Here are two ultimate concerns, interrelated and interacting with each other. The relation of Christian faith and the phenomenon of human life is the interacting, dialectical correlation of ultimates.

One question raised by the current, speedily changing situation of genetics is "What can be done with this knowledge that is ethically acceptable?" That is an urgent question, of course, but it is not the only one raised by genetics. Another is "How does our expanding knowledge of genetics affect or modify our theological understanding of human life and the human person?" We must concentrate on the reciprocity of both questions.

We also have to remember that genetics and theology are not two *simple* categories of knowledge. Each word includes a large cluster of specific elements. Among the various aspects of genetics we can see, first, the investigations into the structure and function of DNA chains, chromosomes, and cells, as well as the ongoing development of recombinant DNA technique. Then come the technical applications of this research: these include processes for the improvement of strains of fruit, vegetables, and grains, and livestock, poultry, and fish; the manufacture of hormones, enzymes, and pharmaceuticals; the analysis of the genetic histories of individual human beings for the purpose of counseling parents-to-be regarding potential dangers to their baby, either before conception or before birth; and the still imperfect technique of modifying human cells and tissues for therapeutic purposes.

The theological body of doctrine to which genetic concerns

may be correlated is also made up of various members. The most relevant of these include the revelation of God in creation, the nature and value of human life, freedom, stewardship, sin, evil, suffering, incarnation, community, renewed creation, and hope.

It is evident, therefore, from the complexity of both genetics and theology — the situation and the message — that we have made only a small beginning in the task of correlating them for purposes of intellectual understanding and practical ethics. This start has been made by study groups of the World Council of Churches and the National Council of Churches, and by individual members of diverse denominations.

Creation

The biblically warranted, traditionally reasoned doctrine of creation is our commonly accepted starting point. Depending upon the mode of expression and interpretation of this doctrine, it can be one of three things: either an affront, a banality, or a profundity.

For a scientific materialist, it is an affront to empirical and rational knowledge. Creation in the literal sense of the word must imply a creating power to bring something out of nothing. That power may belong to a divine Creator or a purposeful cause of creation. These are either denied by scientific materialists or avoided by the confession of agnosticism. Since *nothing* is truly created, chance and necessity are the only causes to discuss. No Creator, no creation!

For an uncritical but piously sincere believer, creation is a banality. Everything that exists is simply ascribed to God's creation, providence, and preservation. Science introduces no challenging data. Everything that happens, whether good or evil, is God's doing. And the age-old debate over the relation of God's power and grace to human freedom of will and action is settled by appeal to divine determinism.

For reflective Christians, such as those who look for the correlation of genetics and theology, the doctrine of creation is a profundity. The profound meaning of creation has several facets. We will briefly examine one of these — origination — before turning to two other important facets of creation.

To be sure, the doctrine of creation does speak of origination: "In the beginning God created . . ." A theory of cosmic origin or *cosmogony* which says that the universe began in the split-second flash of a "big bang" (a trivial name for such an event!) need not contradict the belief that "God said, . . . and it was so." Here the Christian believer speaks in faith where the materialist or skeptic refrains even from asking the forbidden question of primal causation. Neither does a scientific theory of the origin of protein and living cells threaten faith in the God who is "the Lord and Giver of life." Theological truth and scientific truth are not necessarily exclusive or opposed. They may be interactive and complementary, as T. F. Torrance has argued.[4] This same double grasp of two orders of truth applies to the origin of species, to the tremendous evidence for the evolution of all forms of organic life, and to the evolving development of *Homo sapiens*.

The Purpose of Creation

The understanding of *how* God creates is not the same, however, as the belief *that* God creates. If the biblical stories in Genesis seem to be irreconcilable to the findings and theories of the best scientists, the same message can be reformulated in the idiom and insight of science without damage to faith in the Creator. This is because the doctrine of creation is less concerned with the *how* than with the *that;* and it is even more directed to the *why* and *what for* of creation. The theological

4. Thomas F. Torrance, *God and Rationality* (London: Oxford University Press, 1971), p. 91.

sense of creation thus transcends scientific inquiry. As Karl Barth rightly asserted, in biblical faith "the purpose of creation is history."[5] And history has its purpose, which is the realization of God's will for creation through covenant with the human race. This realization requires the movement of history within created space and created time.

Now, what correlation of meaning is there between this very brief sketch of the doctrine of creation and the findings of genetic science? From their side, geneticists are teaching theologians that they must not be content with a pre-1953 concept of the human organism, much less with a pre-twentieth-century one. The decoding of DNA molecules by Francis Crick, Maurice Wilkins, and James Watson in 1953 opened vast new possibilities in our understanding of all biological phenomena, including the human: it resulted in breakthroughs in our understanding of physical processes such as evolution, procreation, embryological gestation, environmental adaption, growth, disease, recuperation, and death, and also in the areas of behavioral and intellectual development and action. Geneticists are saying, in effect, to theologians: "You cannot talk sensibly and credibly about the morality of genetic technology while limited by a naive, uninformed, pre-scientific view of human physiology, psychology, and cellular structure and function." According to those researchers who study them, the thousands of diverse genes have an incomprehensible and astonishing power to determine how our bodies are formed, what kind of persons we become, even how we behave.

Does genetic science thus nullify theological anthropology? Carl Sagan, the popular scientist and ardent belittler of religion, writes: "All life on earth is the same life. There are superficial differences. . . . But deep down at the heart of life, we are, all of us, almost identical — redwoods and nematodes,

5. Karl Barth, *Church Dogmatics,* 3/1 (Edinburgh: T. & T. Clark, 1952), p. 42.

viruses and eagles, slime molds and humans. We are all the expressions of proteins and nucleic acids." As for the unusual achievements of human beings, Sagan is content to say, "Human life is a tribute to the subtlety of matter."[6] Does the discovery of genetic identities between human tissue and that of most other organisms negate the belief in special human creation? No. But it does expand our concept of how the eternal, infinite God has used the marvelous mechanisms of creation to fashion us as we are. It opens new horizons of expectation for the continuing, self-directed evolution of our species in centuries or millennia to come.

Caring for Creation

Another implication of the doctrine of creation is the mandate of human stewardship, or our responsibility to care for, cultivate, and rightly use natural (or created) resources.

A biological reductionist is one who reduces the analysis and explanation of all organisms and processes to physical-chemical reactions. Such reactions, in truth, are what make genes function. A recent variation on reductionism explains all human life in terms of bacteria: we are just "bundles of bacteria." Nevertheless, it is evident and obvious that no scientists, however reductionistic and materialistic, deny the distinctive nature of human beings as compared to other species. And these persons often share the same concern that Christians have for ecological and environmental protection of the earth "and the fulness thereof" — often with crusading zeal — even while they skeptically shrug off the Psalmist's notion that "The earth is the Lord's" (Ps. 24:1).

St. Paul once told Stoic and Epicurean philosophers in Athens that he knew the name of the "unknown god" to whom

---

6. Carl Sagan, "Life," *Encyclopaedia Britannica*, 15th ed. (Chicago: University of Chicago Press, 1974), vol. 10, p. 895.

they had built an altar (Acts 17:23). So, by analogy, Christians know the true reason for ecological stewardship, beyond the simple and superficial one of species survival or of enabling each human being to survive.

Ever since the publication of Lynn White's challenging essay "The Historical Roots of Our Ecological Crisis" (1967), there has been much debate over the burden of guilt that the Bible has been accused of bearing for ecological spoliation.[7] This historian of science placed the blame for much of the destruction of the earth's resources upon the biblical teaching of humanity's dominion over nature. He would have made a valid point if he had meant only that Christians of Western civilization had unjustly justified their raping of the planet by appeal to this human-centered belief. But his charge against the biblical teaching of dominion itself has been adequately refuted by those who explain what dominion was really meant to imply.[8] God's promises to Adam and Noah were not warrants for reckless consumption and consequent destruction. To the contrary, the serious sense of responsibility to God, the Creator, was — and still is — the basis for careful prudence and moderation in tending the earthly garden and thereby serving and caring for human life.

Today we can — we must — consider genetics as a matter of created order, just as much as rivers, oceans, soil, and forests. The genes have been here, expressing themselves, for billions of years. But only in *our* lifetime have they been known to us. For the first time in all of human history, our present generation is provided with the clue to understanding in more and more detail how the body grows and functions, what causes diseases, and how diseases may be checked. Genetic knowledge enables us to

7. Lynn White, "The Historical Roots of Our Ecological Crisis," *Science* 155 (March 1967).

8. For ample discussion of this question see J. Robert Nelson, *Science and Our Troubled Conscience* (Philadelphia: Fortress Press, 1980), p. 73.

recognize the genes, cells, and tissues of our bodies as parts of what we call our environment. It is not as though we human beings exist in complete distinction from all the nonhuman entities, whether inert or living, that constitute our environment. Rather, our intimate genetic relation to all other living matter, as well as our chemical relation to all matter as such, means that we are inherently a part of our own environment.

When a biblical, theological concept of stewardship becomes so powerful as to be a real mandate of our faith, we need to assume stewardship of our very genes. This is a much-expanded idea of environmental ethics, and it has many implications for the kind of healthy life we believe God intends for us.

This idea of genetic ecology may seem strange, fanciful, and strained. It is much easier to be anxiously concerned about sea turtles, whales, snail darters, and wetlands, as well as the air we breathe, than about our genes. And yet we do already talk about the dangers of polluting the whole "gene pool," as though it were an ocean of vitality to be protected — which in a very real sense it is.

These reflections may remind some of us of Teilhard de Chardin's concept of "the inwardness of matter," or of Alfred North Whitehead's process philosophy, or of Charles Birch and John Cobb's linking of life and ecology in *The Liberation of Life*.[9] Wherever else such evolutionary process theology may lead, it is surely consonant with the biblical thinking that is fundamental to a theology of human life.

Incarnation

From the doctrine of creation and its corollary of stewardship we can take a bolder step toward articulating the relation of

9. Charles Birch and John Cobb, *The Liberation of Life* (Cambridge: Cambridge University Press, 1981).

genetics and theology. We can speak realistically of the Incarnation. For emphasis, could we not even refer to "the genes of Jesus"?

The question of Christology has stretched both the rationality and the credulity of Christians since the beginning of Christianity. How can we hold together in paradoxical tension the two natures of Jesus Christ — truly divine, truly human? Both naive belief and theological disputation have persisted through the centuries until now. Whether naive or sophisticated, the tendency to dissolve the paradox of incarnation remains attractive: either a fully spiritualized Christ or a fully materialized Jesus, but not both — such are the temptations.

We may not know any more about the nature of divinity than our ancient predecessors did. The Psalms, the Prophets, the Gospels, and the Epistles speak about God with a profundity and freshness that are ever contemporary. But our scientific knowledge of the cosmos, the earth, its chemistry and physics, and our own human physical identity — all this exceeds in wonder both the ancients' view of creation and their simplistic view of God's act of making the eternal Word become flesh.

Why should so esoteric a doctrine as Christology be brought into the discussion of genetics? Because it illustrates the reciprocity or interaction previously described. It shows how new genetic science can intensify the meaning of Christianity's "central dogma," which is the Incarnation. If the fully divine presence in Jesus Christ is not merely "appearance" or "myth," but individually and genuinely human, then we are obligated to regard the unity of his person as comprehending the very genes of his body tissues. This may not make faith in the doctrine of two natures any easier; but it surely intensifies the seriousness of the acceptance of Christ in his full, authentic humanity.

The three doctrines we have discussed — creation, stewardship, and Christology — are not the only areas in which the dialectical correlation of scientific situation and theological message takes place. There are other applicable doctrines, too, that invite serious thought. These others have to do with sin, evil, and suffering, as well as the redemption and renewal of creation and human life.[10] They provide many points of contact with genetic science and genetic medicine where correlation with theology is perceived.

Gene Therapy

The more we learn of the powers of genetic engineering, both currently practicable and potential, the more we are impelled to think about the nature, meaning, and value of human life. The statement of one prominent researcher illustrates this impulsion. In July 1982, in Washington, D.C., Dr. W. French Anderson, Chief of the Laboratory of Molecular Hematology of the National Institutes of Health, addressed the President's Commission for the Study of Ethical Problems in Medicine and Biomedical and Behavioral Research. The pioneer researcher in gene therapy was expressing his views on human genetic engineering. Suddenly, spontaneously, he exclaimed:

> I want to make a statement of self-revelation, which has been occurring over the last two or three hours. . . . I finally understand, after thinking about this for . . . fifteen years or so, why I feel uneasy about the gene therapy work. . . . Is there anything unique about humans? . . . If there's nothing unique about humans — that's not a *theological* question but a very *real* one. That's what I am nervous about.[11]

10. See J. Robert Nelson, *Human Life: A Biblical Basis for Bioethics* (Philadelphia: Fortress Press, 1984), chap. 6.
11. President's Commission for the Study of Ethical Problems in Medicine and Biomedical and Behavioral Research, Proceedings, Ace-Federal Reporters, Washington, D.C. (July 1982): 115-16.

As if to demonstrate the fact that Anderson's question is not only very real but is essentially *the* theological question, the committee members, with Dr. Morris B. Abram in the chair, found themselves discussing the theology of human life for the next hour. For, as Anderson had said, "If there isn't anything unique about humans, there's nothing wrong with doing gene manipulation."

It is not just human uniqueness as such, however, that requires this warning. In terms of taxonomy, human beings are unique in the same sense that all other species of animal life are unique. It may be perceived that human uniqueness is not merely the singularity found among numerous other species, but that humanity has a unique identity in contrast to all other kinds of organisms. Even so, the particular inviolability of human life is not thus established. What is it, then, that warrants our speaking of the grounding of ethics in the unique value of human life? Or, to put the question more searchingly, how can there be appeal to what we often call the "sacredness" or "sanctity" of human life? Are these words of self-evident validity and cogency? Is life literally "holy"? The well-known philosopher and director of the Hastings Center, Daniel Callahan, thinks that sanctity of life is self-evident. Likewise, sociologist Edward Shils of the University of Chicago agrees that "sanctity" is a concept of a priori validity when applied to all human life. Law and ethics presuppose this value, independently of any particular religious or philosophical sources for the truth. As Shils puts it, "If life is not viewed and experienced as sacred, then nothing else would be sacred."[12]

Persons of religious faith, whose source of knowledge and belief is the Holy Bible, should only welcome this affirmation of life's distinctive value as made by secular humanists.

12. Edward Shils, "The Sanctity of Life," in *Life or Death, Ethics and Options,* ed. D. H. Labby (Seattle: University of Washington Press, 1968), p. 9.

Both religiously minded and secularly minded people are often able to agree on a concept of human sanctity. This implies a basic respect for all human beings, for their civil rights, their personal rights to the care and defense of their bodies and minds, and their proxy rights for dependent relatives who are either small children or incompetent. In short, the sanctity of life as a general rule is the implicit basis of medical and genetic ethics.

Beyond this level of respect for life, however, there is the religious apperception of transcendent, metaphysical, or divinely conferred value of each human life. To affirm that all human beings are made in "the image of God" is not merely a complimentary statement about human sentience, conscience, and rational capability. It is, rather, a testimony to God's creation of each distinct individual through the physiological procreative process, and the establishment of a personal relation to that individual. For Christians, this belief is most highly expressed in its fundamental doctrine of Incarnation: God has entered into creation and human history, from the dimension of eternity to temporality. God honors us by becoming identified through Jesus Christ with all humanity and with every person. It is according to this same faith that the divine will favors the optimal enhancement and fulfillment of each person's earthly existence. Yet we all recognize that God's will is often hindered by the distortions and misuses of human freedom, and by the enigmatic, evil contingencies of living.

Today we are seriously confronting the challenges of genetic manipulation of human cells. There is no angel with a flaming sword to prevent our advance into this field of bio-medical science. To be religious is certainly not to be craven or obtuse about trying something new, even when that something is so potentially disturbing and perplexing as bio-technology. But neither is it an authentically religious mentality if we naively expect a good result from every new scientific technique. Human error, avarice, and malice frustrate and corrupt our finest hopes. No, to be religious ought to mean being utterly realistic about the conditions of life in human society, regarding every person or institution or technical process with neither illusion nor despair.

With respect to human genetic engineering, therefore, this foundation for religious ethics in the literal sanctity of human life can be well expressed in the moral motto of medicine: *Primum non nocere!* First of all, do no harm! And when the indications are not quite clear concerning the effects of novel procedures upon patients, the maxim is: Proceed with much caution!

Much attention has recently been given in both popular news media and scientific journals to the question of the ethical acceptability of human gene therapy. Several distinctions need to be drawn clearly if the point of this discussion is to be understood and rightly appreciated. The first, of course, is the essential, textbook difference between the *somatic* cells, which constitute most of the human body, and the *gametic* or sex cells found in the ova and sperm (these gametic cells are also called *germ line* cells). Dr. David Baltimore, a Nobel Prize winner, is quoted as remarking, "People will never understand the difference between gene therapy of somatic cells and modification of the germ line."[13] Such pessimism may be justified. Even so, in theory it is possible to modify either the somatic cells or the germ line cells in order to cure or eliminate certain genetic diseases. The critical difference inheres, however, in the fact that, once gametes have been changed, their altered characteristics will be irrevocable; they will pass on to all future progeny, whereas somatic cells will die with one's body.

A second distinction, emphasized by Dr. Bernard Davis of Harvard Medical School,[14] is between two kinds of expectation or purpose of genetic modification: (1) medical and

13. *Science* 5, 3 (April 1984): 88.
14. Bernard D. Davis, "Cells and Souls," *New York Times*, 28 June 1983.

therapeutic, or (2) eugenic and political. The first type of genetic modification is for the correction of disease caused by certain abnormally structured genes. The second type, the eugenic, is for improving the traits of individuals and, eventually, of whole populations. But of course, the effect of a therapeutic change *could* also have a slight bearing on the traits of a eugenic quality, or alternatively, a dysgenic quality. This is the distinction that is so widely unrecognized in public discussion. The neglect of it has given rise to much sensational speculation and dispute about creating "perfect people" or engineering a "super-race." At the very least, this view fails to perceive the great difference between diseases that are monogenic in origin (i.e., related to a single gene) and physical traits that are polygenic (i.e., related to or controlled by many genes, and therefore not easily altered). At the most, it exceeds the limits of scientifically considered probability and belongs to fantasy and fiction.

The time is not far off when the first clinical trials will demonstrate whether monogenic diseases in *somatic* or *human body* cells can be corrected. The diseases involved in these trials are relatively rare, but they are the most susceptible to treatment: Lesch-Nyhan disease, which causes severe neurological disorders; ADA deficiency, which causes loss of immunity; and PNP, which is similar to ADA deficiency. The process used is the same as is presently practiced in bone marrow transplants.[15] Genes that are lacking must be supplied to activate indispensable enzymes.

No one is sure, however, about predicting the timetable

15. W. French Anderson, "Human Gene Therapy: Scientific and Ethical Considerations," *Journal of Medicine and Philosophy* 10, 3 (August 1985): 276. Dr. Anderson has achieved positive results in experiments with monkeys. See Anderson, et al., "Expression of Human Adenosine Deaminase in Non-human Primates after Retrovirus-mediated Gene Transfer," *Journal of Experimental Medicine* 166 (July 1987). In 1990 he began experimental human gene therapy clinical trials.

for embryonic *germ line* modification. Nevertheless, scientists and non-scientists alike, who are equally concerned with human life and ethical approbation, must ponder what the future might bring. If some scientists regard these questions as merely speculative or even fictional, there are sufficient numbers of other scientists who put us on long-range guard. We are confronted by therapeutic applications to human beings of recombinant DNA techniques, neither the timing nor the consequences of which we yet know. What is unknown need not frighten us, and it does not yet; but it surely constitutes a warning against reckless advance in research.

Various commentators have compared the implications of recombinant DNA technology to the effects of nuclear fission. The comparison is probably apt and warranted. And one lesson we should learn from that pairing of Promethean techniques is the mandate of much greater alertness and caution about genetic engineering than we as a people have shown toward the releasing of atomic energy. Can we not for once learn from bad experience? How much better would be the condition of our natural environment as well as the health and life of uncounted persons if, forty years ago, there had been adequate caution on the part of scientists, engineers, commercial entrepreneurs, and political officials!

With the upsurge of production of new chemical compounds and plastics four decades ago, we were promised a virtually miraculous resolution of problems in manufacturing, transportation, and agriculture. Who at that time prophesied the present catastrophic conditions of toxic emissions and industrial waste, acid rain, polluted water, and poisoned soil?

In the case of genetic engineering, we still have the opportunity and time to exercise reason, prudence, and restraint. Some say that any application at all of recombinant DNA techniques on human subjects should be strictly limited. Others are content to put limits only on experimentation with gametic cells in humans, at least until such time as sufficiently successful experimentation on higher animals and primates with testing of progeny for mutations had warranted beginning attempts at therapeutic intervention in humans.

Meanwhile, some people see the procedure of germ line gene surgery as the most promising way of curing and eliminating the strains of some of the simple but debilitating genetic diseases. They will increase the pressure of persuasion upon clinical geneticists to intervene with human zygotes. Should this actually prove successful, it would surely be welcomed by all. Who can but cheer for an authenticated cure?

But still we must ask, if such techniques are tried, how long should geneticists wait for the treated individuals to grow up and reproduce before assurance could be given that subsequent, inadvertent mutations had not caused as much distress as the genetic disease that had originally been avoided? There are researchers who believe that, given due time, this can be achieved safely. We can only hope that they are right. In the interest of the human lives that might be affected for better or for worse, we await the disclosure of evidence of their assurance. We who are not scientists but concerned citizens will try to keep informed, and we will express our views as best we can.

The Churches' Response

Concurrent with all these developments, since 1980 the National Council of Churches has pursued a study of genetic engineering.[16] The Council's governing board adopted a policy statement in 1986.[17] It endeavors to show how certain Christian doctrines are related to ethical and theological questions

16. National Council of Churches, Panel on Bioethical Concerns, *Genetic Engineering* (New York: Pilgrim Press, 1984).
17. *Genetic Science for Human Benefit, A Policy Statement* (New York: National Council of Churches, 1986).

about genetics. Not only the creation of humankind "in the image of God" is discussed, but also humanity's stewardship of the rest of creation, human freedom, the enigma of evil, and the idea of sin, as well as the moral mandates of fairness, justice, and love. These doctrines are correlated with several practical issues: medical genetics, counseling and diagnosis, assisted reproduction, pharmaceuticals, and commercial and military biotechnology. Simple pious statements of opinion are avoided as consistently as are overly simple analyses of problems. The critical ambivalence of attitude is well expressed:

> The sudden burst of genetic research and application may well be considered an activity of the divinely endowed mind and spirit of intelligent inquiry and will to serve. But appreciation for scientific achievement is not unconditional, for it is tempered always by humane and ethical considerations, and by awareness that all human endeavor is flawed.[18]

How can the role of religious bodies and their interpreters be assessed in so short a time as they have been active? The Institute of Religion's project on genetics, religion, and ethics — of which the present volume is a part — is keeping up the momentum of inquiry and deliberation among many religious thinkers, scientists, and physicians. Results of two ecumenical study conferences will be made known in 1992. Meanwhile, three observations may be drawn from deliberations of the participants:

1. Consensus has emerged on a basic premise: namely, that the use of genetic engineering on human beings is not a challenge to the veracity of religious beliefs but, rather, a strong stimulus to intelligent correlating of religious doctrines with genetic data as scientifically discerned.

2. The distinctive message of religious thinkers to geneticists is not just "Proceed with caution." Persons of all persua-

18. Ibid.

sions say this. Neither is concern for the value of human life
a uniquely religious disposition. The unique contribution of
biblically based faith is what is called "the hermeneutics of
suspicion." The President's Commission could find no ground
for concluding that "any current or planned forms of genetic
engineering, whether using human or non-human material, are
intrinsically wrong or irreligious per se."[19] This statement
strikes a theologian as being too rationalistic, too sure, too
optimistic about human uses of intellectual and technical skills.

3. The initiatives of churches, synagogues, and individual
persons have definitely served the purpose of keeping scientists, legislators, and the public respectfully aware of both the
critical concerns and the positive contributions of religious
ethicists, theologians, and religious committees. A remarkably
free communication has developed between exponents of religious thought and genetic scientists (many of the latter, of
course, being members of churches and synagogues). Theologians are now almost customarily included in national conferences on genetics. They even participate in — and sometimes
chair — committees of the National Institutes of Health, ad-
vise the Office of the Human Genome Initiative, and publish
essays in leading scientific and medical journals. This unprecedented phenomenon represents a stark contrast to the sepa-
ration of religion and science that many people have either
taken for granted or have desired. Clearly, this is a new era.
Welcome to it!

19. *Splicing Life,* report of the President's Commission for the
Study of Ethical Problems in Medicine and Biomedical and Behavioral
Research (Washington, D.C.: Government Printing Office, 1982), p. 77.

Hope

Gabriel Fackre

FOR ME TO SPEAK about hope in the setting in which this essay was first presented — the Institute of Religion in the Texas Medical Center — was something of a laboratory experiment. As I understand it, the Institute exists to identify the basic issues of life, death, and destiny that happen in the medical workplace. It does this with the people who live and struggle there. Where else then could one better test theological affirmations about hope than among those who are faced daily with its possibilities and perils?

Good theology is done in the midst of our involvement in the workaday world. God struggles and suffers and signals from within that cauldron of living and dying. So we should think with our Bible in one hand and our newspaper in the other, as Karl Barth remarked. For just that reason, as I prepared this essay I tested out these theses on hope with some colleagues who work in places similar to the Texas Medical Center.

My "guinea pigs" are a group of scientists in Boston who have been meeting for nine years, once a month, grappling with how they can responsibly live out their calling in their

83

scientific workplace. They are all connected with Eliot Church in Newton. One month, Arnold Reif may discuss a code of ethics that he has developed for cancer research workers in Boston City Hospital. Another month, Phil Sharp may pose questions about the morality of gene manipulation in the laboratories of MIT. At still another meeting Larry Shaefferr may examine the ethical issues entailed in his work to clean up Boston harbor. For many years this has been a peer support group in the "ministry of the laity." The group has been of incalculable value to the pastor, Herbert Davis, who learns about the realities of the workplace, and in turn shares his theological lore.

As this group of scientists has learned, there are four recurring human puzzlements and agonies: death, suffering, sin, and ignorance. In all times and in every place, people confront them, and their religions and philosophies strive to cope with them.

One or another of these perennial problems seems to come to the fore in a given era. In early Christian history, the inevitable fact of mortality was the dominant question. Human sin was the preoccupation of the late Middle Ages and Reformation, and ignorance was the overriding issue during the eighteenth-century Enlightenment. Today, judging by the movements that capture the hearts and minds of multitudes, the books that flood the market, the topics that pervade radio and TV talk shows, and the religious fervor of the hour, it is suffering that commands our attention. The ravages of history seem more perilous than ever with the threat of nuclear or ecological disaster. But the raised awareness of the good things that some have and others do not, or the contrast between what we all might have but do not yet have, sharpens our sense of deprivation and therefore our demand for justice, health, peace, and plenty. Away with suffering!

For each of these four cries for release a response is given. For death, life; for sin, forgiveness; for ignorance, truth. And for suffering? Hope! Desmond Tutu has captured this well in his book title as well as in his life: *Hope and Suffering*.[1] And the present volume, *Life as Liberty, Life as Trust*, rightly concludes with the subject of hope. What sense would it make for Robert Drinan to challenge world hunger if he had no hope? For Jim Wallis to call evangelicals to a life of suffering, if there was no hope? For Roy Sano to open vistas to a world without racism, or for Robert Jewett to speak about the eschatology of the New Testament, without hope? What sense would it make for Robert Nelson's Institute of Religion to engage the perplexing medical and biomedical issues arising today if it did not have a hope for tomorrow? Living toward the future means hoping in the future. And especially in our time, and in every place, there is a universal *cri de coeur*, a pleading for some credible word of hope. Do we have such a word?

A Range of Hopes

There are serious hopes, and then there are hopes that are more foolish, idle, or fanciful. Consider the following examples of the wide range of meanings *hope* can have:

(1) "I hope it doesn't rain next week during our picnic." In this common usage hope is simply *desire*. We want something to happen in the future because it fits our agenda, but there is really no basis for the hoped-for circumstance, not even the evening TV weather forecast. Hoping here is merely "wishful thinking."

(2) "I hope there will be no earthquake in Massachusetts next year." Well, this is a wish too. But it seems to be of a different order. There seems to be some basis for this hope, since earthquakes are quite rare in New England; the chances

1. Desmond Tutu, *Hope and Suffering* (Grand Rapids: Eerdmans, 1984).

of this unwished-for event happening seem slender. But the people on the West Coast keep telling us not to rest secure! There *have* been earthquakes in New England before. Indeed, I felt a rumble in our living room just last year. So hoping here has an "iffy" quality, as in the first case. It is still wishing, but in this case there is the hint of a warrant for wishing.

(3) In the fall of 1989, someone said, "I have hope that East Germany will hold free elections in 1990." Notice what has happened in this usage: first, *hope* has shifted from a verb to a noun; and second, some hard evidence lies behind the hope — the events taking place in East Germany at that time. Hoping is still uncertain in this case. Things could have changed; the old socialist order could have reasserted itself. But events were unfolding that constituted a *trajectory into the future.* There was a good chance that things anticipated would come true.

Paul Tillich once observed that what distinguishes hope from wishful thinking is precisely this trajectory from the present into the future. In the case of East Germany, evidence of momentum in 1989 was a portent of things to come. We had a kind of trajectory from the present in the case of our "no earthquake in New England" hope, too, but there the trajectory was only *latent,* while in the case of East Germany it is *patent.* The reality and patency of the trajectory into the future account for the shift from a verb to a noun.

Now let us return to our Boston scientists. They were very clear on this point of distinguishing hope that is supported by hard evidence from hope that is less certain or that is even mere wishful thinking. They worried about the facile claims made for new discoveries and new cures. They spoke of the temptation to overstate a case without due regard for the evidence in seeking foundation grants or newspaper headlines. Hope in the laboratory must be *warranted* hope, clearly grounded in hard-won experimental data. Such hope is still not certain, but it is much more likely.

(4) "We have . . . a sure and steadfast anchor of the soul, a hope that enters into the inner shrine" (Heb. 6:19). The symbol implied in these words is a familiar and traditional one in church architecture — the anchor of hope. We have now moved from all degrees of "iffyness" to a "sure and steadfast" hope, an anchor thrown out to the waves of the future and solidly secured.

Notice, however, where the anchor has landed: in the absolute future, the World to Come. This is the Great Hope at the end of history, not a sure thing inside history, not a utopian expectation for our plans and projects in the here and now. This Great Hope has to do with the promise that a day is coming when the wolf will lie down with the lamb, swords will be beaten into plowshares, every flaw will be mended, and the prayer of Christ will come true: the Kingdom will come and God's will shall be done. To live out of that kind of confidence changes everything.

We need to look more keenly into *why* this hope can be a noun, and why there is such confidence associated with it. It has to do with the relation of hope to a sister virtue, faith: "Faith is the assurance of things hoped for, the conviction of things not seen" (Heb. 11:1). The anchor of hope is attached to a sturdy chain that reaches into the depths. This is a "theology of hope" that we must presently explore. For now, we will continue to delineate a typology of hope.

Turning once again to our list of examples, notice the similarities between scientific and religious hoping (numbers 3 and 4). Both require evidence that warrants future expectations. But the character of the evidence differs. One comes from the eyes of sight, and the other from the eyes of faith. The evidence of one carries the caution proper to its discipline, while the evidence of the other carries a confidence proper to its field of inquiry.

For all the differences in the data, the similarities are striking. While Christian hoping is grounded in the evidence provided by faith, it is not "blind faith." To be sure, it entails a "leap" made possible only by the grace of God and not by knock-down arguments. But this leap of faith is taken from a running start on terrain that is discernible by anyone willing to see with the "eyes of sight." Christian faith honors the evidence of the scientific laboratory and the medical journal in its own journey. It believes that God "did not leave himself without witness" (Acts 14:17) in the world at large, and in human experience in general. Even here there is a hint of hope, given by a Christ hidden in the poor and needy of the world (see Matt. 25:40). Karl Menninger, a person of faith as well as scientific insight, helps us to see this overlap in his own research, summarized in a famous presidential address to the American Psychiatric Association entitled "Hope."[2] To this essay we will now turn.

Vain and Valid Hope

Menninger begins his investigation by surveying some of the critics of hope in the history of philosophy and literature. Euripides (echoing Solon, Pindar, Aeschylus, Simonides, and Thucydides) put it simply: Hope is humanity's "curse." Succeeding thinkers expressed opinions equally dubious: "Hope-fortune's cheating lottery, where for one prize a hundred blanks go by" (Cowley); "Worse than despair, worse than the bitterness of death, is hope" (Shelley); "Hope is the worst of evils, for it prolongs the torment of man" (Nietzsche).[3] Thus early Greek fatalism continued in the popular cynicisms and nihilisms of a later day.

Menninger argues that doubt about hope continues today in the minds of physicians and psychiatrists. In both

2. Karl Menninger, "Hope," in *Sparks,* ed. Lucy Freeman (New York: Thomas Y. Crowell, 1973), pp. 81-97.
3. Cited in ibid., p. 85.

cases this is understandable — such restraint derives from a history filled with good reasons for repressing hope. Doctors have fought a long battle to bring their profession out of the morass of human ignorance and magic. They want to honor hard facts, to pursue careful diagnosis, to resist the imposter's claim to a quick fix, to let realism control what is wished for. That means refusing to offer a false "straw of hope" to the desperate patient who believes that doctors have godlike powers, and who craves assurances that the data do not warrant.

> Every physician in the world has heard the devil whispering. "Command that these stones become bread. . . . All these things I will give thee if thou wilt fall down and . . ." And sometimes he falls down. He exploits the patient's hope.[4]

False hope is worse than no hope. A good doctor, like a good pastor, helps people face the facts of living and dying. The art of such a ministry in both cases has to do with *discernment:* where and when are the doors open or closed to the future? The possibilities and the impossibilities? It is no accident that the prayer of one pastor, Reinhold Niebuhr, has meant so much to so many:

> God, give us grace to accept with serenity the things that cannot be changed, courage to change the things which should be changed, and the wisdom to distinguish the one from the other.

While neither pastor nor doctor can be part of a conspiracy of silence before the facts, there have been too many unchallenged assumptions about what constitutes "the facts." This is the burden of Menninger's message to people of the helping professions: the future is much more open than

4. Ibid., p. 91.

simplistic scientific closures and medical taciturnity have allowed. We have been too quick to counsel acceptance of a status quo that "in fact" *is* changeable . . . by hope. We have been too ready to be servile before presumed fact.

To make his case, Menninger piles evidence upon evidence: he tells of one case after another in which apparently hopeless patients recovered because of their will to live; he also tells of many cases in which a good prognosis was frustrated because of a will to die. The determining factor in each case was the presence or absence of hope. Even in animals the same dynamic appears to be at work; the maze with no perceived way out frustrates and drains off the mysterious powers of life.

Menninger's insights are important not only for the evidence he has adduced but also for the framework within which he scrutinizes that evidence. It is commonly recognized in scientific circles today that imagination is critical to investigation. Menninger has constantly searched for the role of hope in healing.

Our group of Boston scientists, who read and discussed Menninger's essay, were quite definite on the role of imagination in scientific inquiry. Laboratory hypotheses must arise in the right as well as the left hemisphere of the brain — the ability to dream of possibilities that *might be* is a necessary companion to the study of facts that *are*. Imagination is the sister of hope, opening up new paths of investigation.

Menninger's anterior vision that gave impetus to his research was actually a theology of hope. His deep religious convictions were at work in his belief that healing and hope are inextricable. What is this classical Christian view of things to come?

A Theology of Hope

Biblical religion is the antithesis of Greek fatalism and Nietz-schean despair. The reason for this lies in its narrative character. Christian faith is a story that marches purposefully toward a Great End. Consider its plot.

It begins in eternity. "In the beginning was the Word, and the Word was with God . . ." (John 1:1). In other words, God had a Dream! The Greek word *Logos,* usually translated as "Word," had 1300 meanings in ancient times: purpose, plot, vision, dream, hope — and, of course, word — to name a few. So this verse could also be translated, "In the beginning was the *Hope* . . ." Hope for what? Hope for a Life Together like God is. We are talking now about the Christian doctrine of the Trinity. God as three Persons in One is absolute mutuality. In the simple words of 1 John 4:8: "God is love," a loving Life Together.

What God is, God hopes for or wills. The Hope of God is Life Together. So begins chapter 1 in our story: creation. God wills a world of life together, a world in partnership with God. We might portray this invitation to or hope for life together with God as the reach of God toward the world.

But chapter 2 in our story is a collision of hope with reality — the world's "No!" to God's outstretched hand. Sin is the fist shaken in the face of God, the estrangement that replaces partnership. Hope is dashed.

Yet in this story we have to do with a special kind of hope, a *stubborn* hope that is not servile before fact, a "hope against hope." In the next chapter, the covenant with Israel, God makes a commitment to a people that they will be "a light to the nations," that in them and through them God's Hope will be realized.

And so the center of the Christian story is the Word incarnate, the eternal Hope of God, who "became flesh and dwelt among us . . . ; [and] we have beheld his glory, glory as

of the only Son from the Father" (John 1:14). In the midst of
the terrors and turbulence of our reality came God's loving
Purpose, utterly vulnerable to our hates and hurts.

What can we expect from such an encounter other than
what came to be? Is the crucifixion proof that Euripides was
correct in calling hope a curse? Not quite. For the chapter does
not end there. At the heart of this story is other evidence for
those who have the eyes to see: Easter. For Christian faith, the
whole tale of hope turns on that event. Resurrection means that
the worst the world could do to the Purpose of God was not
enough to defeat it. Easter is Hope validated, Hope alive and
well. So Christians are not afraid to use as their central symbol
a Roman instrument of execution and hopelessness, because it
has been emptied of its victim; the Cross is not the victor.

The rest of the story — with chapters on the church,
salvation, and consummation — unfolds as the history of
humanity advances. The church is the community of hope that
tells the story by word and deed. The message is salvation, the
evidences in personal and social history of the healing of the
brokenness brought by sin. And it all looks forward to consummation, when the promise and portents of fulfillment given
in Christ come to fruition, when the Kingdom finally comes,
when ultimate as well as penultimate Hope is fulfilled, when
"God [is] all in all" (1 Cor. 15:28, NIV).

Telling and Hoping

To live by this story is to see things differently. Because God
is a Hoper who has turned the tide right at the center of the
story, we have a right to look on life expectantly. It is no
accident that researchers find in the human heart a will to hope.
From the beginning — at creation — God plants deep inside
of us an aspiration for the divine Purpose. Theology calls it
the *imago Dei*. We are made in the image of God's own Life
Together. Our stumble and fall into the state of sin damages

but does not destroy it. God preserves that hope in us to keep the story moving forward to its goal.

"Our hearts are restless until they find their rest in thee," Augustine confessed to God. And we are not the only ones with that restless hope, "for the whole creation has been groaning in travail" (Rom. 8:22), in the birth pangs of hope. So it is possible to find the urge to hope even in a caged mouse, and perhaps also in the patterns of mutuality in the universe discerned by the philosophies of Teilhard de Chardin or Alfred North Whitehead. Here is the point of contact between human experience and the Christian story. That is why faith is not *blind* faith. So the work of Menninger points to the *empirical* evidence: the futility of vain hopes and the persuasiveness of valid ones.

There are times when it seems we do not have to argue the case for hope. Is now one of those times when hopes have burst out on all sides and long-standing hopes have been vindicated? We think of *glasnost, perestroika,* Poland, Hungary, East Germany, Czechoslovakia, Rumania. The hope mills of God grind slowly, but exceeding fine. The human spirit, sculpted by the Holy Spirit, cannot give up hoping and acting toward it. The *imago Dei* lives.

Yes, hope is everywhere, and rightly so. But there is yet another lesson to be learned from our story. The Easter event at the center of the story gives us a right to hope, but not a right to *presumption.* Presumption is utopian hope, naivete, groundless hope, wishful thinking. Presumption declares confidently that right here and now "I'm OK, you're OK." And as for tomorrow, "Don't worry, be happy!" Even the hopes bursting out in Eastern Europe can be presumptive, romanticized. Indeed, some of the ambiguities in these advances can already be seen. Today's ambiguities and horrors and tomorrow's terrors are better served by a *sober* hope. Sobriety in the story means that in this world, short of the coming of the final *shalom,* the perfect Kingdom of God, there is much toil and trouble and no quick fix. As it is said, "Christ reigns, *but from a cross.*"

Sometimes Jewish believers must remind Christians of the "not yet" dimension of their own hoping. We say Hope has come in Jesus. But then the Holocaust has come, too, in spite of Jesus. Where then is the hope? Our answer can only be that with Jews we are "partners in waiting." The Finale is yet to be, when hopes are perfectly fulfilled. All presumption and utopias are put into question by the crucifixion. And the Holocaust confirms the sobriety of hope, as do the bones broken in movements for the freedom of oppressed people. But for Christians, the hope that will be fulfilled only at the End is firmly planted in the Hope that has already come in Galilee, on Calvary, and on Easter morning.

How much can we hope for in human history? That question is often debated among believing Christians. Some say we will get only a whiff of the Final Banquet in this life, or perhaps just an aperitif. Others say we may get more — soup and salad, perhaps, or maybe even the main course. And a few, the utopians still among us, believe we can expect the whole Great Meal, dessert included. A sober hope, I believe, will stick close to biblical texts that speak of signs, portents, firstfruits — a taste of things to come, modest but not inordinate claims.

But the most important thing on which all Christians agree is the surety of hope in God's ultimate victory through Jesus Christ over the temptations of futility and fatalism. God

> will wipe away every tear from their eyes, and death shall be no more, neither shall there be mourning nor crying nor pain any more, for the former things have passed away. (Rev. 21:4)

These sure and steadfast words, spoken regularly at burial services, are why *hope* is a noun in the Christian vocabulary. Here is the anchor lodged firmly in the Future. We know it is there because we have seen it with the eyes of faith.

> Faith is the assurance of things hoped for, the conviction of things not seen. (Heb. 11:1)

And Paul adds:

> Hope that is seen is not hope. For who hopes for what he
> sees? But if we hope for what we do not see, we wait for it
> with patience. (Rom. 8:24-25)

Mobilizing Hope

The wise and very familiar words of the book of Proverbs
declare, "Where there is no vision, the people perish" (29:18,·
KJV). Proverbs is part of the "wisdom literature" of the Hebrew Scriptures: sayings that contain universally recognizable
and accessible truths. As we have been noting, there are evidences in human experience, from the laboratories of the heart
and of the hospital, that point to the importance of hope.
Without it people really do perish. Hopelessness breeds death.

The counterpart of that in Christian faith is the mobilizing power of Christian hope. Such mobilizing hope is active
in very personal matters of life and death and also in larger
social contexts. Epochal moments of renewal, reformation, and
revolution have been fueled by Christian hope. Not so long
ago we experienced such a burst of energy in the North American churches, generated by the great dreamer and hoper,
Martin Luther King, Jr.

"I have a dream . . . !"

King's vision was rooted in his confidence that the Kingdom
is coming, that it is breaking into history. And that means a
time is coming when black and white children can walk hand
in hand on the red earth of Georgia and over the molehills of
Mississippi. We would have no hope that these things could
happen if we had no faith that the battle has already been won
in Jesus Christ. Despair *paralyzes,* but hope *mobilizes!*

Karl Barth put it in the code language of faith when he

wrote to British Christians who were enduring Hitler's devastating bomb attacks:

> The world in which we live is the place where Jesus Christ rose from the dead. . . . Since this is true, the world . . . is not some sinister wilderness where fate or chance holds sway, or where all sorts of "principalities and powers" run riot unrestrained and rage about unchecked. . . . The Kingly Rule of Christ extends not merely over the Church . . . but, regardless of whether men believe or not, over the whole of the universe in all its heights and depths; and it also confronts and overrules with sovereign dignity the principalities and powers and evil spirits of this world. . . . We Christians . . . have no right whatsoever to fear and respect them. . . . We should be slighting the resurrection of Jesus Christ . . . if we forgot that the world in which we live is already consecrated, and if we did not, for Christ's sake, come to grips spiritedly and resolutely with these evil spirits.[5]

These powerful cadences had an effect on British readers' determination to "resist the powers." Easter hope propels believers into action. It has the same power today in our struggles for peace, ecological survival, and justice for the oppressed. But this faith is also fundamental in quieter times and places, including our day-to-day decision making in laboratories and operating rooms, and by beds of pain and death. Apostles of hope believe . . . and act.

> So we do not lose heart. . . . For this slight momentary affliction is preparing for us an eternal weight of glory beyond all comparison, . . . for the things that are seen are transient, but the things that are unseen are eternal. (2 Cor. 4:16-18)

5. Karl Barth, *A Letter to Great Britain from Switzerland* (London: Sheldon Press, 1941), pp. 9-11.